THE PERMANENT REVOLUTION

LEON TROTSKY

ISBN: 978-1495497230

Table of Contents

THE PERMANENT REVOLUTION

INTRODUCTION TO THE RUSSIAN EDITION

This book is devoted to an issue which is intimately linked with the history of the three Russian Revolutions. But not with that history alone. This issue has played an enormous role in recent years in the internal struggle in the Communist Party of the Soviet Union; it was then carried into the Communist International, played a decisive role in the development of the Chinese Revolution and determined a whole number of most important decisions on problems bound up with the revolutionary struggle of the countries of the East. This issue has to do with the theory of the permanent revolution, which, according to the teachings of the epigones of Leninism (Zinoviev, Stalin, Bukharin, etc.) represents the original sin of 'Trotskyism'.

The question of the permanent revolution was once again raised in 1924 after a long interval and, at first sight, quite unexpectedly. There was no political justification for it; it was a matter of differences of opinion which belonged to the distant past. But there were important psychological motives. The group of so-called 'old Bolsheviks' who had opened up a fight against me began by counter posing themselves to me as the 'Bolshevik Old Guard'. But a great obstacle in their path was the year 1917. However important may have been the preceding history of ideological struggle and preparation, nonetheless, not only with regard to the party as a whole but also with regard to different individuals, this whole preceding preparatory period found its highest and categorical test in the October Revolution. *Not a single one of the epigones stood up under this test.* Without exception, they all at the time of the February 1917 Revolution adopted the vulgar position of democratic Left Wingers. Not a single one of them raised the slogan of the workers' struggle for power. They all regarded the course toward a socialist revolution as absurd or—still worse—as 'Trotskyism'. In this spirit they led the party up to the time of Lenin's arrival from abroad and the publication of his famous April Theses. After this, Kamenev, already in direct struggle against Lenin, openly tried to form a democratic wing of Bolshevism. Later he was joined by Zinoviev, who had arrived with Lenin. Stalin, heavily compromised by his social-patriotic position, stepped to the sidelines. He let the party forget his miserable articles and speeches of the decisive March weeks and gradually edged over to Lenin's standpoint. This is why the question automatically arose: What had any of these leading 'old Bolsheviks' got from Leninism when not a single one of them showed himself capable of applying independently the theoretical and practical experiences of the party at a most important and most critical historical moment? Attention had to be diverted from this question at all costs and another question substituted for it. To this end, it was decided to concentrate fire on the permanent revolution. My adversaries did not, of course, foresee that in creating an artificial axis of struggle they would imperceptibly be compelled to revolve it around themselves and to manufacture, by the method of inversion, a new world outlook for themselves.

In its essential features, the theory of the permanent revolution was formulated by me even before the decisive events of 1905. Russia was approaching the bourgeois revolution. No one in the ranks of the Russian Social Democrats (we all called ourselves Social Democrats then) had any doubts that we were approaching a bourgeois revolution, that is, a revolution produced by the contradictions between the development of the productive forces of capitalist society and the outlived caste and state relationships of the period of serfdom and the Middle Ages. In the struggle against the Narodniks and the anarchists, I had to devote not a few speeches and articles in those days to the Marxist analysis of the bourgeois character of the impending revolution.

The bourgeois character of the revolution could not, however, answer in advance the question of which classes would solve the tasks of the democratic revolution and what the mutual relationships of these classes would be. It was precisely at this point that the fundamental strategic problems began.

Plekhanov, Axelrod, Zasulich, Martov and, following them, all the Russian Mensheviks, took as their point of departure the idea that to the liberal bourgeoisie, as the natural claimant to power, belong the leading role in the bourgeois revolution. According to this pattern, the party of the proletariat was assigned the role of Left Wing of the democratic front. The Social Democrats were to support the liberal bourgeoisie against the reaction and at the same time to defend the interests of the proletariat against the liberal bourgeoisie. In other words, the **Mensheviks** understood the bourgeois revolution principally as a liberal-constitutional reform.

Lenin posed the question in an altogether different manner. For Lenin, the liberation of the productive forces of bourgeois society from the fetters of serfdom signified, first and foremost, a radical solution of the agrarian question in the sense of complete liquidation of the landowning class and revolutionary redistribution of landownership. Inseparably connected with this was the destruction of the monarchy. Lenin attacked the agrarian problem, which affected the vital interests of the overwhelming majority of the population and at the same time constituted the basic problem of the capitalist market, with a truly revolutionary boldness. Since the liberal bourgeoisie, which confronts the worker as an enemy, is intimately bound by innumerable ties to large landed property, the genuine democratic liberation of the peasantry can be realized only by the revolutionary co-operation of the workers and peasants. According to Lenin, their joint uprising against the old society must, if victorious, lead to the establishment of the 'democratic dictatorship of the proletariat and peasantry'.

This formula is now repeated in the Communist International as a sort of supra-historical dogma, with no attempt to analyze the living historical experiences of the last quarter-century—as though we had not been witnesses and participants in the Revolution of 1905, the February Revolution of 1917, and finally the October Revolution. Such a historical analysis, however, is all the more necessary because never in history has there been a regime of the 'democratic dictatorship of the proletariat and peasantry'.

In 1905, it was a question with Lenin of a strategic hypothesis still to be verified by the actual course of the class struggle. The formula of the democratic dictatorship of the proletariat and peasantry bore in large measure an intentionally algebraic character. Lenin did not solve in advance the question of what the political relationships would be between the two participants in the assumed democratic dictatorship, that is, the proletariat and the peasantry. He did not exclude the possibility that the peasantry would be represented in the revolution by an independent party—a party independent in a double sense, not only with regard to the bourgeoisie but also with regard to the proletariat, and at the same time capable of realizing the democratic revolution in alliance with the party of the proletariat in struggle against the liberal bourgeoisie. Lenin even allowed the possibility—as we shall soon see—that the revolutionary peasants' party might constitute the majority in the government of the democratic dictatorship.

In the question of the decisive significance of the agrarian revolution for the fate of our bourgeois revolution, I was, at least from the autumn of 1902, that is, from the time of my first flight abroad, a pupil of Lenin's. That the agrarian revolution, and consequently, the general democratic revolution also, could be realized only by the united forces of the workers and the peasants in struggle against the liberal bourgeoisie, was for me, contrary to all the senseless fairy tales of recent years, beyond any doubt. Yet I came out against the formula 'democratic dictatorship of the proletariat and the peasantry', because I saw its shortcoming in the fact that it left open the question of which class would wield the real dictatorship. I endeavored to show that in spite of its enormous social and revolutionary weight the peasantry was incapable of creating a really independent party and even less capable of concentrating the revolutionary power in the hands of such a party. Just as in the old revolutions, from the German Reformation of the sixteenth century, and even before that, the peasantry in its up-risings gave support to one of the sections of the urban bourgeoisie and not infrequently ensured its victory, so, in our belated bourgeois revolution, the peasantry might at the peak of its struggle extend similar support to the proletariat and help it to come to power. From this I drew the conclusion that our bourgeois revolution could solve its tasks radically only in the event that the proletariat, with the aid of the multi-million peasantry, proved capable of concentrating the revolutionary dictatorship in its own hands.

What would be the social content of this dictatorship? First of all, it would have to carry through to the end the agrarian revolution and the democratic reconstruction of the State. In other words, the dictatorship of the proletariat would become the instrument for solving the tasks of the historically-belated bourgeois revolution. But the matter could not rest there. Having reached power the proletariat would be compelled to encroach even more deeply upon the relationships of private property in general, that is to take the road of socialist measures.

'But do you really believe,' the Stalins, Rykovs and all the other Molotovs objected dozens of times between 1905 and 1917, 'that Russia is ripe for the socialist revolution?' To that I always answered:

No, I do not. But world economy as a whole and European economy in the first place, is fully ripe for the socialist revolution. Whether the dictatorship of the proletariat in Russia leads to socialism or not, and at what tempo and through what stages, will depend upon the fate of European and world capitalism.

These were the essential features of the theory of the permanent revolution at its origin in the early months of 1905. Since then, three revolutions have taken place. The Russian proletariat rose to power on the mighty wave of the peasant insurrection. The dictatorship of the proletariat became a fact in Russia earlier than in any of the immeasurably more developed countries of the world. In 1924, that is, no more than seven years after the historical prognosis of the theory of the permanent revolution had been confirmed with quite exceptional force, the epigones opened up a frenzied attack against this theory, plucking isolated sentences and polemical rejoinders out of old works of mine which I had by then completely forgotten.

It is appropriate to recall here that the first Russian revolution broke out more than half a century after the wave of bourgeois revolutions in Europe and thirty-five years after the episodic uprising of the Paris Commune. Europe had time to grow unaccustomed to revolutions. Russia had not experienced any. All the problems of the revolution were posed anew. It is not difficult to understand how many unknown and conjectural magnitudes the future revolution held for us in those days. The formulae of all the groupings were, each in their own way, working hypotheses. One must have complete incapacity for historical prognosis and utter lack of understanding of its methods in order now, after the event, to consider analyses and evaluations of 1905 as though they were written yesterday. I have often said to myself and to my friends: I do not doubt that my prognoses of 1905 contained many defects which it is not hard to show up now, after the event. But did my critics see better and further? Not having re-read my old works for a long time, I was ready in advance to admit to defects in them more serious and important than really were there. I became convinced of this in 1928, when the political leisure imposed upon me by exile in Alma- Ata gave me the opportunity to re-read, pencil in hand, my old writings on the problems of the permanent revolution. I hope that the reader, too, will be thoroughly convinced of this by what he reads in the pages that follow.

It is nevertheless necessary, within the limits of this introduction, to present as exact as possible a characterization of the constituent elements of the theory of the permanent revolution, and the most important objections to it. The dispute has so broadened and deepened that it now embraces in essence all the most important questions of the world revolutionary movement.

The permanent revolution, in the sense which Marx attached to this concept, means a revolution which makes no compromise with any single form of class rule, which does not stop at the democratic stage, which goes over to socialist measures and to war against reaction from without: that is, a revolution whose every successive stage is rooted in the preceding one and which can end only in the complete liquidation of class society.

To dispel the chaos that has been created around the theory of the permanent revolution, it is necessary to distinguish three lines of thought that are united in this theory.

First, it embraces the problem of the transition from the democratic revolution to the socialist. This is in essence the historical origin of the theory.

The concept of the permanent revolution was advanced by the great Communists of the middle of the nineteenth century, Marx and his co-thinkers, in opposition to the democratic ideology which, as we know, claims that with the establishment of a 'rational' or democratic state all questions can be solved peacefully by reformist or evolutionary measures. Marx regarded the bourgeois revolution of 1848 as the direct prelude to the proletarian revolution. Marx 'erred'. Yet his error has a factual and not a methodological character. The Revolution of 1848 did not turn into the socialist revolution. But that is just why it also did not achieve democracy. As to the German Revolution of 1918, it was no democratic completion of the bourgeois revolution, it was a proletarian revolution decapitated by the Social Democrats; more correctly, it was a bourgeois counter-revolution, which was compelled to preserve pseudo-democratic forms after its victory over the proletariat.

Vulgar 'Marxism' has worked out a pattern of historical development according to which every bourgeois society sooner or later secures a democratic regime, after which the proletariat, under conditions of democracy, is gradually organized and educated for socialism. The actual transition to socialism has been variously conceived: the avowed reformists pictured this transition as the reformist filling of democracy with a socialist content (Jaures); the formal revolutionists acknowledged the inevitability of applying revolutionary violence in the; transition to socialism (Guesde). But both the former and the latter considered democracy and socialism, for all peoples and countries, as two stages in the development of society which are not only entirely distinct but also separated by great distances of time from each other. This view was predominant also among those Russian Marxists who, in the period of 1905, belonged to the Left Wing of the Second International. Plekhanov, the brilliant progenitor of Russian Marxism, considered the idea of the dictatorship of the proletariat a delusion in contemporary Russia. The same standpoint was defended not only by the Mensheviks but also by the overwhelming majority of the leading Bolsheviks, in particular by those present party leaders, without exception, who in their day were resolute revolutionary democrats but for whom the problems of the socialist revolution, not only in 1905 but also on the eve of 1917, still signified the vague music of a distant future.

The theory of the permanent revolution, which originated in 1905, declared war upon these ideas and moods. It pointed out that the democratic tasks of the backward bourgeois nations lead directly, in our epoch, to the dictatorship of the proletariat and that the dictatorship of the proletariat puts socialist tasks on the order of the day. Therein lay the central idea of the theory. While the traditional view was that the road to the dictatorship of the proletariat led through a long period of democracy, the theory of the permanent revolution established the fact that for backward countries the road to democracy passed through the dictatorship of the proletariat. Thus democracy is not a regime that remains self-sufficient for decades, but is only a direct prelude to the socialist revolution. Each is bound to the other by an unbroken chain. Thus there is established between the democratic revolution and the socialist reconstruction of society a permanent state of revolutionary development.

The second aspect of the 'permanent' theory has to do with the socialist revolution as such. For an indefinitely long time and in constant internal struggle, all social relations undergo transformation. Society keeps on changing its skin. Each stage of transformation stems directly from the preceding. This process necessarily retains a political character, that is, it develops through collisions between various groups in the society which is in transformation. Outbreaks of civil war and foreign wars alternate with periods of 'peaceful' reform. Revolutions in economy, technique, science, the family, morals and everyday life develop in complex reciprocal action and do not allow society to achieve equilibrium. Therein lays the permanent character of the socialist revolution as such.

The international character of the socialist revolution, which constitutes the third aspect of the theory of the permanent revolution, flows from the present state of economy and the social structure of humanity. Internationalism is no abstract principle but a theoretical and political reflection of the character of world economy, of the world development of productive forces and the world scale of the class struggle. The socialist revolution begins on national foundations—but it cannot be completed within these foundations. The maintenance of the proletarian revolution within a national framework can only be a provisional state of affairs, even though, as the experience of the Soviet Union shows, one of long duration. In an isolated proletarian dictatorship, the internal and external contradictions grow inevitably along with the successes achieved. If it remains isolated, the proletarian state must finally fall victim to these contradictions. The way out for it lies only in the victory of the proletariat of the advanced countries. Viewed from this standpoint, a national revolution is not a self-contained whole; it is only a link in the international chain. The international revolution constitutes a permanent process, despite temporary declines and ebbs.

The struggle of the epigones is directed, even if not always with the same clarity, against all three aspects of the theory of the permanent revolution. And how could it be otherwise, when it is a question of three inseparably connected parts of a whole? The epigones mechanically separate the *democratic* and the *socialist* dictatorships. They separate the *national* socialist revolution from the *international*. They consider that, in essence, the conquest of power within national limits is not the initial act but the final act of the revolution; after that follows the period of reforms that lead to the national socialist society. In 1905, they did not even grant the idea that the proletariat could conquer power in Russia earlier than in Western Europe. In 1917, they preached the self-sufficing democratic revolution in Russia and spurned the dictatorship of the proletariat. In 1925-27, they steered a course toward national revolution in China under the leadership of the national bourgeoisie. Subsequently, they raised the slogan for China of the democratic dictatorship of the workers and peasants in opposition to the slogan of the dictatorship of the proletariat. They proclaimed the possibility of the construction of an isolated and self-sufficient socialist society in the Soviet Union. The world revolution became for them, instead of an indispensable condition for victory, only a favorable circumstance. This profound breach with Marxism was reached by the epigones in the process of permanent struggle against the theory of the permanent revolution.

The struggle, which began with an artificial revival of historical reminiscences and the falsification of the distant past, led to the complete transformation of the world outlook of the ruling stratum of the revolution. We have already repeatedly explained that this re-evaluation of values was accomplished under the influence of the social needs of the Soviet bureaucracy, which became ever more conservative, strove for national order and demanded that the already-achieved revolution, which insured privileged positions to the bureaucracy, should now be considered adequate for the peaceful construction of socialism. We do not wish to return to this theme here. Suffice it to note that the bureaucracy is deeply conscious of the connection of its material and ideological positions with the theory of *National Socialism*. This is being expressed most crassly right now, in spite of, or rather because of, the fact that the Stalinist machine of government, under the pressure of contradictions which it did not foresee, is driving to the left with all its might and inflicting quite severe blows upon its Right-Wing inspirers of yesterday. The hostility of the bureaucrats toward the Marxist Opposition, whose slogans and arguments they have borrowed in great haste, is not, as we know, diminishing in the least. The condemnation of the theory of the permanent revolution, and an acknowledgment, even if only indirect, of the theory of socialism in one country, is demanded, first and foremost, of those Oppositionists who raise the question of their re-admission into the party for the purpose of supporting the course toward industrialization, etc. By this the Stalinist bureaucracy reveals the purely *tactical* character of its left turn which goes along with retention of its national-reformist *strategic* foundations. It is superfluous to explain what this means; in politics as in war, tactics are in the long run subordinated to strategy.

The question has long ago gone beyond the specific sphere of the struggle against 'Trotskyism'. Gradually extending itself, it has to-day embraced literally all the problems of the revolutionary world outlook. Either permanent revolution or socialism in one country—this alternative embraces at the same time the internal problems of the Soviet Union, the prospects of revolution in the East, and finally, the fate of the Communist International as a whole.

The present work does not examine this question from all these sides; it is not necessary to repeat what has been already said in other works. In the *Criticism of the Draft Program of the Communist International*, I have endeavored to disclose theoretically the economic and political untenability of National Socialism. The theoreticians of the Comintern have kept mum about this. That is indeed the only thing left for them to do. In this book I above all restore the theory of the permanent revolution as it was formulated in 1905 with regard to the internal problems of the Russian revolution. I show wherein my position actually differed from Lenin's, and how and why it coincided with Lenin's position in every decisive situation. Finally, I endeavor to reveal the decisive significance of this question for the proletariat of the backward countries, and thereby for the Communist International as a whole.

What charges have been brought against the theory of the permanent revolution by the epigones? If we discard the innumerable contradictions of my critics, then their entire and truly vast body of writing can be reduced to the following propositions:

1. Trotsky ignored the difference between the bourgeois revolution and the socialist revolution. Already in 1905 he considered that the proletariat of Russia was directly faced with the tasks of a socialist revolution.

2. Trotsky completely forgot the agrarian question. The peasantry did not exist for him. He depicted the revolution as a matter of single combat between the proletariat and Tsarism.

3. Trotsky did not believe that the world bourgeoisie would tolerate for any length of time the existence of the dictatorship of the Russian proletariat, and regarded its downfall as inevitable unless the proletariat of the West seized power within a very short period and came to our assistance. Thereby Trotsky underestimated the pressure of the Western European proletariat upon its own bourgeoisie.

4. Trotsky does not in general believe in the power of the Russian proletariat, in its ability to construct socialism independently; and that is why he has put and still puts all his hopes in the international revolution.

These motifs run through not only the numberless writings and speeches of Zinoviev, Stalin, Bukharin and others, but they are also formulated in the most authoritative resolutions of the Communist Party of the Soviet Union and the Communist International. And in spite of that, one is compelled to say that they are based upon a mixture of ignorance and dishonesty.

The first two contentions of the critics are, as will be shown later on, false to the very roots. No, I proceeded precisely from the bourgeois-democratic character of the revolution and arrived at the conclusion that the profundity of the agrarian crisis could raise the proletariat of backward Russia to power. Yes, this was precisely the idea I defended on the eve of the 1905 Revolution. This was precisely the idea that was expressed by the very designation of the revolution as a 'permanent', that is, an uninterrupted one, a revolution passing over directly from the bourgeois stage into the socialist. To express the same idea Lenin later used the excellent expression of the bourgeois revolution growing over into the socialist. The conception of 'growing over' was counter posed by Stalin, after the event (in 1924), to the permanent revolution, which he presented as a direct leap from the realm of autocracy into the realm of socialism. This ill-starred 'theoretician' did not even bother to ponder the question: What meaning can there be to the *permanency* of the revolution, that is, its *uninterrupted* development, if all that is involved is a mere leap?

As for the third accusation, it was dictated by the short-lived faith of the epigones in the possibility of *neutralizing* the *imperialist* bourgeoisie for an unlimited time with the aid of the 'shrewdly' organized pressure of the proletariat. In the years 1924-27, this was Stalin's central idea. The Anglo-Russian Committee was its fruit. Disappointment in the possibility of binding the world bourgeoisie hand and foot with the help of Purcell, Radic, LaFollette and Chiang Kai-shek led to an acute paroxysm of fear of an immediate war danger. The Comintern is still passing through this period.

The fourth objection to the theory of the permanent revolution simply amounts to saying that I did not in 1905 defend the standpoint of the theory of socialism in one country which Stalin first manufactured for the Soviet bureaucracy in 1924. This accusation is a sheer historical curiosity. One might actually believe that my opponents, insofar as they thought politically at all in 1905, were of the opinion then that Russia was ripe for an independent socialist revolution. As a matter of fact, in the period 1905-17 they were tireless in accusing me of utopianism because I allowed the probability that the Russian proletariat could come to power before the proletariat of Western Europe. Kamenev and Rykov accused Lenin of utopianism in April 1917, and therewith they explained to Lenin in simple language that the socialist revolution must first be achieved in Britain and in the other advanced countries before it could be Russia's turn. The same standpoint was defended by Stalin, too, up to April 4, 1917. Only gradually and with difficulty did he adopt the Leninist formula of the dictatorship of the proletariat in contradistinction to the democratic dictatorship. In the spring of 1924, Stalin was still repeating what others had said before him: taken separately, Russia is not ripe for the construction of a socialist society. In the autumn of 1924, Stalin, in his struggle against the theory of the permanent revolution, for the first time discovered the possibility of building an isolated socialism in Russia. Only then did the Red Professors collect quotations for Stalin which convicted Trotsky of having believed in 1905—how terrible!—that Russia could reach socialism only with the aid of the proletariat of the West.

Were one to take the history of the ideological struggle over a period of a quarter-century, cut it into little pieces, mix them in a mortar, and then command a blind man to stick the pieces together again, a greater theoretical and historical jumble of nonsense could hardly result than the one with which the epigones feed their readers and hearers.

To illumine the connection of yesterday's problems with today's, one must recall here, even if only very generally, what the leadership of the Comintern, that is, Stalin and Bukharin, perpetrated in China.

Under the pretext that China was faced with a national liberationist revolution, the leading role was allotted in 1924 to the Chinese bourgeoisie. The party of the national bourgeoisie, the Kuomintang, was officially recognized as the leading party. Not even the Russian Mensheviks went that far in 1905 in relation to the Cadets (the party of the liberal bourgeoisie).

But the leadership of the Comintern did not stop there. It compelled the Chinese Communist Party to enter the Kuomintang and submit to its discipline. In special telegrams from Stalin, the Chinese Communists were urged to curb the agrarian movement. The workers and peasants rising in revolt were forbidden to form their own soviets in order not to alienate Chiang Kai-shek, whom Stalin defended against the Oppositionists as a 'reliable ally' at a party meeting in Moscow at the beginning of April, 1927, that is, a few days before the counter-revolutionary coup D'etat in Shanghai.

The official subordination of the Communist Party to the bourgeois leadership, and the official prohibition of forming soviets (Stalin and Bukharin taught that the Kuomintang 'took the place' of soviets), was a grosser and more glaring betrayal of Marxism than all the deeds of the Mensheviks in the years 1905 -1917.

After Chiang Kai-shek's coup D'etat in April, 1927, a Left Wing, under the leadership of Wang Ching-wei, split off temporarily from the Kuomintang. Wang Ching-wei was immediately hailed in *Pravda* as a reliable ally. In essence, Wang Ching-wei bore the same relation to Chiang Kai-shek as Kerensky to Milyukov, with this difference that in China Milyukov and Kornilov were united in the single person of Chiang Kai-shek.

After April, 1927, the Chinese party was ordered to enter the 'Left' Kuomintang and to submit to the discipline of the Chinese

Kerensky instead of preparing open warfare against him. The 'reliable' Wang Ching-wei crushed the Communist Party, and together with it the workers' and peasants' movement, no less brutally than Chiang Kai-shek, whom Stalin had declared his reliable ally.

Though the Mensheviks supported Milyukov in 1905 and afterwards, they nevertheless did not enter the liberal party. Though the Mensheviks went hand in hand with Kerensky in 1917, they still retained their own organization. Stalin's policy in China was a malicious caricature even of Menshevism. That is what the first and most important chapter looked like.

After its inevitable fruits had appeared—complete decline of the workers' and peasants' movement, demoralization and breakup of the Communist Party—he leadership of the Comintern gave the command: "Left about turn!" and demanded immediate transition to the armed uprising of the workers and peasants. Up to yesterday the young, crushed and mutilated Communist Party still served as the fifth wheel in the wagon of Chiang Kai-shek and Wang Ching-wei, and consequently lacked the slightest independent political experience. And now suddenly this party was commanded to lead the workers and peasants—whom the Comintern had up to yesterday held back under the banner of the Kuomintang—in an armed insurrection against the same Kuomintang which had meanwhile found time to concentrate the power and the army in its hands. In the course of 24 hours a fictitious soviet was improvised in Canton. An armed insurrection, timed in advance for the opening of the Fifteenth Congress of the Communist Party of the Soviet Union, expressed simultaneously the heroism of the advanced Chinese workers and the criminality of the Comintern leaders. Lesser adventures preceded the Canton uprising and followed it. Such was the second chapter of the Chinese strategy of the Comintern. It can be characterized as the most malicious caricature of Bolshevism. The liberal- opportunist and adventurist chapters delivered a blow to the Chinese Communist Party from which, even with a correct policy, it can only recover after a number of years.

The Sixth Congress of the Comintern drew up the balance sheet of all this work. It gave it unreserved approval. This is hardly surprising, since the Congress was convoked for this purpose. For the future, the Congress advanced the slogan 'democratic dictatorship of the proletariat and peasantry.' Wherein this dictatorship would differ from the dictatorship of the Right or Left **Kuomintang**, on the one side, and the dictatorship of the proletariat on the other—this was not explained to the Chinese Communists. Nor is it possible to explain it.

Proclaiming the slogan of the democratic dictatorship the Sixth Congress at the same time condemned democratic slogans as impermissible (constituent assembly, universal suffrage, freedom of speech and of the press, etc.) and thereby completely disarmed the Chinese Communist Party in the face of the dictatorship of the military oligarchy. For a long number of years, the Russian Bolsheviks had mobilized the workers and peasants around democratic slogans. Democratic slogans played a big role in 1917. Only after the Soviet power had actually come into existence and clashed politically with the Constituent Assembly, irreconcilably and in full view of the entire people, did our party liquidate the institutions and slogans of formal democracy, that is, bourgeois democracy, in favor of real soviet democracy, that is, proletarian democracy.

The Sixth Congress of the Comintern, under the leadership of Stalin and Bukharin, turned all this upside down. While on the one hand it prescribed the slogan of 'democratic' and not 'proletarian' dictatorship for the party, it simultaneously forbade it to use democratic slogans in preparing for this dictatorship. The Chinese Communist Party was not only disarmed, but stripped naked. By way of consolation it was finally permitted in the period of unlimited domination of the counter-revolution, to use the slogan of soviets, which had remained under ban throughout the upsurge of the revolution. A very popular hero of Russian folk-lore sings wedding songs at funerals and funeral hymns at weddings. He is soundly thrashed on both occasions. If what was involved was only thrashings administered to the strategists of the incumbent leadership of the Comintern, one might perhaps reconcile oneself to it. But much greater issues are at stake. Involved here is the fate of the proletariat. The tactics of the Comintern constituted an unconsciously, but all the more reliably, organized sabotage of the Chinese Revolution. This sabotage was accomplished with certainty of success, for the Right Menshevik policy of 1924-27 was clothed by the Comintern with all the authority of Bolshevism, and at the same time was protected by the Soviet power, through its mighty machine of repression, from the criticism of the Left Opposition.

As a result, we saw accomplished a finished experiment of Stalinist strategy, which proceeded from beginning to end under the flag of a struggle against the permanent revolution. It was, therefore, quite natural that the principal Stalinist theoretician of the subordination of the Chinese Communist Party to the national-bourgeois Kuomintang should have been Martynov. This same Martynov had been the principal Menshevik critic of the theory of the permanent revolution from 1905 right up to 1923, the year when he began to fulfill his historic mission in the ranks of Bolshevism.

The essential facts about the origin of the present work are dealt with in the first chapter. In Alma-Ata I was unhurriedly preparing a theoretical polemic against the epigones. The theory of the permanent revolution was to occupy a large place in this book. While at work, I received a manuscript by Radek which was devoted to counter posing the permanent revolution to the strategic line of Lenin. Radek needed to make this, so to say, unexpected sortie because he was himself submerged up to his ears in Stalin's Chinese policy: Radek (together with Zinoviev) defended the subordination of the Communist Party to the Kuomintang not only before Chiang Kai-shek's coup D'etat but even after it.

To provide a basis for the enslavement of the proletariat to the bourgeoisie, Radek naturally cited the necessity of an alliance with the peasantry and my 'underestimation' of this necessity. Following Stalin, he too defended Menshevik policy with Bolshevik phraseology. With the formula of the democratic dictatorship of the proletariat and the peasantry, Radek, following Stalin, once again covered up the fact that the Chinese proletariat had been diverted from independent struggle for power at the head of the peasant masses. When I exposed this ideological masquerade, there arose in Radek the urgent need to prove that my struggle against opportunism disguising itself with quotations from Lenin was derived in reality from the contradiction between the theory of the permanent revolution and Leninism. Radek, speaking as attorney in defense of his own sins, converted his speech into a prosecutor's indictment of the permanent revolution. This served him only as a bridge to capitulation. I had all the more reason to suspect this since Radek, years before, had planned to write a pamphlet in defense of the permanent revolution. Still I did not hasten to write Radek off. I tried to answer his article frankly and categorically without at the same time cutting off his retreat. I print my reply to Radek just as it was written, confining myself to a few explanatory notes and stylistic corrections.

Radek's article was not published in the press, and I believe it will not be published, for in the form in which it was written in 1928 it could not pass through the sieve of the Stalinist censorship. Even for Radek himself this article would be downright fatal today, for it would give a clear picture of his ideological evolution, which very strongly recalls the 'evolution' of a man who throws himself out of a sixth-floor window.

The origin of this work explains sufficiently why Radek occupies a larger place in it than it is perhaps his right to claim. Radek did not think up a single new argument against the theory of the permanent revolution. He came forward only as an epigone of the epigones. The reader is, therefore, recommended to see in Radek not simply Radek but the representative of a certain corporation, in which he purchased an associate membership at the price of renouncing Marxism. Should Radek personally feel that too many digs have fallen to his share, then he should at his own discretion turn them over to the more appropriate addresses. That is the private affair of the firm. For my part, I raise no objections.

Various groupings of the German Communist Party have come into power or fought for it by demonstrating their qualifications for leadership by means of critical exercises against the permanent revolution. But this entire literature, emanating from Maslow, Thalheimer and the rest, is on such a sorry level that it does not even provide a pretext for a critical answer. The Thaelmanns, the Remmeles and other incumbent leaders by appointment, have taken this question even a stage lower. All these critics have succeeded merely in demonstrating that they are unable to reach even the threshold of the question. For this reason, I leave them—beyond the threshold. Anyone interested in the theoretical critiques by Maslow, Thalheimer and the rest, can, after reading this book, turn to their writings in order to convince himself of the ignorance and dishonesty of these authors. This will be, so to speak, a by-product of the work I am offering the reader.

L. TROTSKY

INTRODUCTION TO THE GERMAN EDITION

As this book goes to press in the German language, the entire thinking section of the world working class and, in a sense, the whole of 'civilized' humanity is following with particularly keen interest the economic turn, and its reverberations, now taking place over most of the former Tsarist Empire. The greatest attention in this connection is aroused by the problem of collectivizing the peasant holdings. This is hardly surprising: in this sphere the break with the past assumes a particularly sweeping character. But a correct evaluation of collectivization is unthinkable without a general conception of the socialist revolution. And here, on a much higher plane, we once again become convinced that in the field of Marxist theory there is nothing that fails to impinge on practical activity. The most remote, and it would seem, the most 'abstract' disagreements, if they are thought out to the end, will sooner or later be invariably expressed in practice, and practice does not allow a single theoretical mistake to be made with impunity.

The collectivization of peasant holdings is, of course, a most necessary and fundamental part of the socialist transformation of society. However, the scope and tempo of collectivization are not determined by the government's will alone, but, in the last analysis, by the economic factors: by the height of the country's economic level, by the inter-relationship between industry and agriculture, and consequently by the technical resources of agriculture itself.

Industrialization is the driving force of the whole of modern culture and by this token the only conceivable basis for socialism. In the conditions of the Soviet Union, industrialization means first of all the strengthening of the base of the proletariat as a ruling class. Simultaneously it creates the material and technical premises for the collectivization of agriculture. The tempos of these two processes are interdependent. The proletariat is interested in the highest possible tempos for these processes to the extent that the new society in the making is thus best protected from external danger, and at the same time a source is created for systematically improving the material level of the toiling masses.

However, the tempos that can be achieved are limited by the general material and cultural level of the country, by the relationship between the city and the village and by the most pressing needs of the masses, who are able to sacrifice their today for the sake of tomorrow *only up to a certain point*. The optimum tempos, i.e., the best and most advantageous ones, are those which not only promote the most rapid growth of industry and collectivization at a given moment, but which also secure the necessary stability of the social regime, that is, first of all strengthen the alliance of the workers and peasants, thereby preparing the possibility for future successes.

From this standpoint, of decisive significance is the general historical criterion in accordance with which the party and state leadership direct economic development by means of planning. Here two main variants are possible: (a) the course outlined above toward the economic strengthening of the proletarian dictatorship in one country until further victories of the world proletarian revolution (the viewpoint of the Russian Left Opposition); and (b) the course toward the construction of an isolated national socialist society, and this 'in the shortest possible time' (the current official position).

These are two completely different, and, in the last analysis, directly opposed conceptions of socialism. From these are derived basically different lines, strategy and tactics.

In the limits of this preface we cannot deal in detail with the question of building socialism in one country. To this we have devoted a number of writings, particularly *Criticism of the Draft Program of the Comintern*. Here we confine ourselves to the fundamental elements of this question. Let us recall, first of all, that the theory of socialism in one country was first formulated by Stalin in the autumn of 1924, in complete contradiction not only to all the traditions of Marxism and the school of Lenin, but even to what Stalin himself had written in the spring of the same year. From the standpoint of principle, the departure from Marxism by the Stalinist 'school' on the issues of socialist construction is no less significant and drastic than, for example, the break of the German Social Democrats from Marxism on the issues of war and patriotism in the fall of 1914, exactly ten years before the Stalinist turn. This comparison is by no means accidental in character. Stalin's 'mistake', just like the 'mistake' of the German Social Democracy, is *National Socialism*.

Marxism takes its point of departure from world economy, not as a sum of national parts but as a mighty and independent reality which has been created by the international division of labor and the world market, and which in our epoch imperiously dominates the national markets. The productive forces of capitalist society have long ago outgrown the national boundaries. The imperialist war (of 1914-1918) was one of the expressions of this fact. In respect of the technique of production socialist society must represent a stage higher than capitalism. To aim at building a nationally isolated socialist society means, in spite of all passing successes, to pull the productive forces backward even as compared with capitalism. To attempt, regardless of the geographical, cultural and historical conditions of the country's development, which constitutes a part of the world unity, to realize a shut-off proportionality of all the branches of economy within a national framework, means to pursue a reactionary utopia. If the heralds and supporters of this theory nevertheless participate in the international revolutionary struggle (with what success is a different question) it is because, as hopeless eclectics, they mechanically combine abstract internationalism with reactionary utopian national socialism. The crowning expression of this eclecticism is the program of the Comintern adopted by the Sixth Congress.

In order to expose graphically one of the main theoretical mistakes underlying the national socialist conception we cannot do better than quote from a recently published speech of Stalin, devoted to the internal questions of American Communism. **(1)** 'It would be wrong,' says Stalin, arguing against one of the American factions, 'to ignore the specific peculiarities of American capitalism. The Communist party must take them into account in its work. But it would be still more wrong to base the activities of the Communist party on these specific features, since the foundation of the activities of every Communist party, including the American Communist Party, on which it must base itself, must be the *general* features of capitalism, which are the *same for all countries*, and not its specific features in any given country. *It is precisely on this that the internationalism of the Communist parties rests.* The specific features are merely *supplementary* to the general features.' (Bolshevik, No. 1, 1930, p. 8. Our emphasis.).

These lines leave nothing to be desired in the way of clarity. Under the guise of providing an economic justification for internationalism, Stalin in reality presents a justification for National Socialism. It is false that world economy is simply a sum of national parts of one and the same type. It is false that the specific features are 'merely supplementary to the general features,' like warts on a face. In reality, the national peculiarities represent an original combination of the basic features of the world process. This originality can be of decisive significance for revolutionary strategy over a span of many years. Suffice it to recall that the proletariat of a backward country has come to power many years before the proletariat of the advanced countries. This historic lesson alone shows that in spite of Stalin, it is absolutely wrong to base the activity of the Communist parties on some 'general features', that is, on an abstract type of national capitalism. It is utterly false to contend that 'this is what the internationalism of the Communist parties rests upon'. In reality, it rests on the insolvency of the national state, which has long ago outlived itself and which has turned into a brake upon the development of the productive forces. National capitalism cannot be even understood, let alone reconstructed, except as a part of world economy.

The economic peculiarities of different countries are in no way of a subordinate character. It is enough to compare England and India, the United States and Brazil. But the specific features of national economy, no matter how great, enter as component parts and in increasing measure into the higher reality which is called world economy and on which alone, in the last analysis, the internationalism of the Communist parties rests.

Stalin's characterization of national peculiarities as a simple 'supplement" to the general type, is in crying and therewith not accidental contradiction to Stalin's understanding (that is, his lack of understanding) of the law of uneven development of capitalism. This law, as is well known, is proclaimed by Stalin as the most fundamental, most important and universal of laws. With the help of the law of uneven development, which he has converted into an empty abstraction, Stalin tries to solve all the riddles of existence. But the astonishing thing is that he does not notice that *national peculiarity is nothing else but the most general product of the unevenness of historical development, its summary result, so to say*. It is only necessary to understand this unevenness correctly, to consider it in its full extent, and also to extend it to the pre-capitalist past. A faster or slower development of the productive forces; the expanded, or, contrariwise, the contracted character of entire historical epochs—for example, the Middle Ages, the guild system, enlightened absolutism, parliamentarism; the uneven development of different branches of economy, different classes, different social institutions, different fields of culture—all these lie at the base of these national 'peculiarities'. The peculiarity of a national social type is the crystallization of the unevenness of its formation.

The October Revolution came as the most momentous manifestation of the unevenness of the historic process. The theory of the permanent revolution gave the prognosis of the October Revolution; by this token this theory rested on the law of uneven development, not in its abstract form, but in its material crystallization in Russia's social and political peculiarity.

Stalin has dragged in the law of uneven development not in order to foresee in time the seizure of power by the proletariat of a backward country, but in order, after the fact, in 1924, to foist upon the already victorious proletariat the task of constructing a national socialist society. But it is precisely here that the law of uneven development is inapplicable, for it does not replace nor does it abolish the laws of world economy; on the contrary, it is subordinated to them.

By making a fetish of the law of uneven development, Stalin proclaims it a sufficient basis for National Socialism, not as a type common to all countries, but exceptional, Messianic, purely Russian. It is possible, according to Stalin, to construct a self-sufficient socialist society only in Russia. By this alone he elevates Russia's national peculiarities not only above the 'general features' of every capitalist nation, but also above world economy as a whole. It is just here that the fatal flaw in Stalin's whole conception begins. The peculiarity of the U.S.S.R. is so potent that it makes possible the construction of its own socialism within its own borders, regardless of what happens to the rest of mankind. As regards other countries, to which the Messianic seal has not been affixed, their peculiarities are merely 'supplementary' to the general features, only a wart on the face. 'It would be wrong,' teaches Stalin, 'to base the activities of the Communist parties on these specific features'. This moral holds good for the American C.P., and the British, and the South African and the Serbian, but—not for the Russian, whose activity is based not on the 'general features' but precisely on the 'peculiarities.' From this flows the thoroughly dualistic strategy of the Comintern. While the U.S.S.R. 'liquidates the classes' and builds socialism, the proletariat of all the other countries, in complete disregard of existing national conditions, is obligated to carry on uniform activity according to the calendar (First of August, March Sixth, etc.). Messianic nationalism is supplemented by bureaucratically abstract internationalism. This dualism runs through the whole program of the Comintern, and deprives it of any principled significance.

If we take Britain and India as polarized varieties of the capitalist type, then we are obliged to say that the internationalism of the British and Indian proletariats does not at all rest on an *identity* of conditions, tasks and methods, but on their indivisible *interdependence*. Successes for the liberation movement in India presuppose a revolutionary movement in Britain and vice versa. Neither in India, nor in England is it possible to build an *independent* socialist society. Both of them will have to enter as parts into a higher whole. Upon this and only upon this rests the unshakable foundation of Marxist internationalism.

Recently, on March 8, 1930, *Pravda* expounded anew Stalin's ill-starred theory, in the sense that 'socialism, as a social-economic formation,' that is, as a definite system of production relations, can be fully realized 'on the national scale of the U.S.S.R.' Something else again is 'the *final victory of socialism*' in the sense of a guarantee against the intervention of capitalist encirclement—such a final victory of socialism 'actually demands the triumph of the proletarian revolution in several advanced countries.' What an abysmal decline of theoretical thought was required for such shoddy scholasticism to be expounded with a learned air in the pages of the central organ of Lenin's party! If we assume for a minute the possibility of realizing socialism as a finished social system within the isolated framework of the U.S.S.R., then that would be the 'final victory'—because in that case what talk could there be about a possible intervention? The socialist order presupposes high levels of technology and culture and solidarity of population. Since the U.S.S.R., at the moment of complete construction of socialism, will have, it must be assumed, a population of between 200,000,000 and 250,000.000, we then ask: What intervention could even be talked of then? What capitalist country, or coalition of countries, would dare think of intervention in these circumstances? The only conceivable intervention could come from the side of the U.S.S.R. But would it be needed? Hardly. The example of a backward country, which in the course of several Five-Year Plans was able to construct a mighty socialist society with its own forces, would mean a death blow to world capitalism, and would reduce to a minimum, if not to zero, the costs of the world proletarian revolution. This is why the whole Stalinist conception actually leads to the liquidation of the Communist International. And indeed, what would be its historical significance, if the fate of socialism is to be decided by the highest possible authority—the State Planning Commission of the U.S.S.R.? In that case, the task of the Comintern, along with the notorious 'Friends of the Soviet Union,' would be to protect the construction of socialism from intervention, that is, in essence, to play the role of frontier patrols.

The article mentioned attempts to prove the correctness of the Stalinist conception with the very newest and freshest economic arguments: '.... Precisely now, 'says *Pravda*, 'when productive relations of a socialist type are taking deeper root not only in industry but also in agriculture through the growth of state farms, through the gigantic rise, quantitatively and qualitatively, of the collective-farm movement and the liquidation of the kulaks as a class on the basis of complete collectivization, precisely now what is shown dearest of all is the sorry bankruptcy of the Trotskyite-Zinovievite theory of defeat, which has meant in essence "the Menshevik denial of the legitimacy of the October Revolution" (Stalin)'. (*Pravda*, March 8, 1930.)

These are truly remarkable lines, and not merely for their glib tone which covers a complete confusion of thought. Together with Stalin, the author of *Pravda*'s article accuses the 'Trotskyite' conception of 'denying the legitimacy of the October Revolution.' But it was exactly on the basis of this conception, that is, the theory of the permanent revolution, that the writer of these lines *foretold the inevitability* of the October Revolution, thirteen years before it took place. And Stalin? Even after the February Revolution, that is seven to eight months prior to the October Revolution; he came forward as a vulgar revolutionary democrat. It was necessary for Lenin to arrive in Petrograd (April 3, 1917) with his merciless struggle against the conceited 'Old Bolsheviks,' whom Lenin ridiculed so at that time, for Stalin carefully and noiselessly to glide over from the democratic position to the socialist. This inner 'growing over' of Stalin, which by the way was never completed, took place, at any rate, not earlier than 12 years after I had offered proof of the 'legitimacy' of the seizure of power by the working class of Russia before the beginning of the proletarian revolution in the West.

But, in elaborating the theoretical prognosis of the October Revolution, I did not at all believe that, by conquering state power, the Russian proletariat would exclude the former Tsarist Empire from the orbit of world economy. We Marxists know the role and meaning of state power. It is not at all a passive reflection of economic processes, as the Social Democratic servants of the bourgeois state depict it. Power can have a gigantic significance, reactionary as well as progressive, depending on which class holds power in its hands. But state power is nonetheless an instrument of the super structural order. The passing of power from the hands of Tsarism and the bourgeoisie into the hands of the proletariat abolishes neither the processes nor the laws of world economy. To be sure, for a certain time after the October Revolution, the economic ties between the Soviet Union and the world market were weakened. But it would be a monstrous mistake to make a generalization out of a phenomenon that was merely a brief stage in the dialectical process. The international division of labor and the supra-national character of modern productive forces not only retain but will increase twofold and tenfold their significance for the Soviet Union in proportion to the degree of Soviet economic ascent.

Every backward country integrated with capitalism has passed through various stages of decreasing or increasing dependence upon the other capitalist countries, but in general the tendency of capitalist development is toward a colossal growth of world ties, which is expressed in the growing volume of foreign trade, including, of course, capital export. Britain's dependence upon India naturally bears a qualitatively different character from India's dependence upon Britain. But this difference is determined, at bottom, by the difference in the respective levels of development of their productive forces, and not at all by the degree of their economic self- sufficiency. India is a colony; Britain, a metropolis. But if Britain were subjected today to an economic blockade, it would perish sooner than would India under a similar blockade. This, by the way, is one of the convincing illustrations of the reality of world economy.

Capitalist development—not in the abstract formulas of the second volume of *Capital*, which retain all their significance as a *stage in analysis*, but in historical reality—took place and could only take place by a systematic expansion of its base. In the process of its development, and consequently in the struggle with its internal contradictions, every national capitalism turns in an ever-increasing degree to the reserves of the 'external market,' that is, the reserves of world economy. The uncontrollable expansion growing out of the permanent internal crises of capitalism constitutes a progressive force up to the time when it turns into a force fatal to capitalism.

Over and above the internal contradictions of capitalism, the October Revolution inherited from old Russia the contradictions, no less profound, between capitalism as a whole and the pre-capitalist forms of production. These contradictions possessed, as they still do, a material character, that is, they are embodied in the material relations between town and country, they are lodged in the particular proportions or disproportions between the various branches of industry and in the national economy as a whole, etc. Some of the roots of these contradictions lie directly in the geographical and demographical conditions of the country, that is, they are nurtured by the abundance or scarcity of one or another natural resource, the historically-created distribution of the masses of the population, and so on. The strength of Soviet economy lies in the nationalization of the means of production and their planned direction. The weakness of Soviet economy, in addition to the backwardness inherited from the past, lies in its present post-revolutionary isolation, that is, in its inability to gain access to the resources of world economy, not only on a socialist but even on a capitalist basis, that is, in the shape of normal international credits and 'financing' in general, which plays so decisive a role for backward countries. Meanwhile, the contradictions of the Soviet Union's capitalist and pre-capitalist past not only do not disappear of themselves, but on the contrary rise up from the recovery from the years of decline and destruction; they revive and are aggravated with the growth of Soviet economy, and in order to be overcome or even mitigated they demand at every step that access to the resources of the world market be achieved.

To understand what is happening now in the vast territory which the October Revolution awakened to new life, it is necessary to take clearly into account that to the old contradictions recently revived by the economic successes there has been added a new and most powerful contradiction between the concentrated character of Soviet industry, which opens up the possibility of unexampled tempos of development, and the isolation of Soviet economy, which excludes the possibility of a normal utilization of the reserves of world economy. The new contradiction, pressing down upon the old ones, leads to this, that alongside of tremendous successes, painful difficulties arise. These find their most immediate and onerous expression, felt daily by every worker and peasant, in the fact that the conditions of the toiling masses do not keep step with the general rise of the economy, but are even growing worse at present as a result of the food difficulties. The sharp crises of Soviet economy are a reminder that the productive forces created by capitalism are not adapted to national markets, and can be socialistically coordinated and harmonized only on an international scale. To put it differently, the crises of Soviet economy are not merely maladies of growth, a sort of infantile sickness, but something far more significant—namely, they are the harsh curbing of the world market, the very one 'to which,' in Lenin's words, 'we are subordinated, with which we are bound up, and from which we cannot escape.' (Speech at the Eleventh Party Congress, March 27, 1922). From the foregoing, however, there in no way follows a denial of the historical 'legitimacy' of the October Revolution, a conclusion which reeks of shameful philistinism. The seizure of power by the international proletariat cannot be a single, simultaneous act. The political superstructure—and a revolution is part of the 'superstructure'—has its own dialectic, which intervenes imperiously in the process of world economy, but does not abolish its deep-going laws. The October Revolution is 'legitimate' as the *first stage of the world revolution* which unavoidably extends over decades. The interval between the first and the second stage has turned out to be considerably longer than we had expected. Nevertheless it remains an interval, and it is by no means converted into a self-sufficient epoch of the building of a national socialist society. Out of the two conceptions of the revolution there stem two guiding lines on (Soviet) economic questions. The first swift economic successes, which were completely unexpected by Stalin, inspired him in the fall of 1924 with the theory of socialism in one country as the culmination of the practical prospect of an isolated national economy. It was precisely in

31

this period that Bukharin advanced his famous formula that by protecting ourselves from world economy by means of the monopoly of foreign trade, we should be in a position to build socialism 'although at a tortoise pace.' This was the common formula of the bloc of the Centrists (Stalin) with the Rights (Bukharin). Already at that time, Stalin tirelessly propounded the idea that the tempo of our industrialization is our 'own affair,' having no relation whatever to world economy. Such a national smugness naturally could not last long, for it reflected the first, very brief stage of economic revival, which necessarily revived our dependence on the world market. The first shocks of international dependence, unexpected by the national socialists, created an alarm, which in the next stage turned into panic. We must gain economic 'independence' as speedily as possible with the aid of the speediest possible tempos of industrialization and collectivization!—this is the transformation that has taken place in the economic policy of National Socialism in the past two years. Creeping and penny-pinching was replaced all along the line by adventurism. The theoretical base under both remains the same: the national socialist conception.

The basic difficulties, as has been shown above, derive from the objective situation, primarily from the isolation of the Soviet Union. We shall not pause here to consider to what extent this objective situation is itself a product of the subjective mistakes of the leadership (the false policy in Germany in 1923, in Bulgaria and Estonia in 1924, in Britain and Poland in 1926, in China in 1925-27; the current false strategy of the 'Third Period,' etc., etc.). But the sharpest convulsions in the U.S.S.R. are created by the fact that the incumbent leadership tries to make a virtue out of necessity, and out of the political isolation of the workers' state constructs a program of an economically-isolated socialist society. This has given rise to the attempt at complete socialist collectivization of peasant holdings on the basis of a pre-capitalist inventory—a most dangerous adventure which threatens to undermine the very possibility of collaboration between the proletariat and the peasantry.

Remarkably, just at the moment when this has become delineated in all its sharpness, Bukharin, yesterday's theoretician of the 'tortoise pace,' has composed a pathetic hymn to the present-day 'furious gallop' of industrialization and collectivization. It is to be feared that this hymn, too, will presently be declared the greatest heresy. For there are already new melodies in the air. Under the influence of the resistance of economic reality, Stalin has been compelled to beat a retreat. Now the danger is that yesterday's adventurist offensive, dictated by panic, may turn into a panic-stricken retreat. Such alternation of stages results inexorably from the nature of National Socialism.

A realistic program for an isolated workers' state cannot set itself the goal of achieving 'independence' from world economy, much less of constructing a national socialist society 'in the shortest time.' The task is not to attain the abstract maximum tempo, but the optimum tempo, that is, the best, that which follows from both internal and world economic conditions, strengthens the position of the proletariat, prepares the national elements of the future international socialist society, and at the same time, and above all, systematically improves the living standards of the proletariat and strengthens its alliance with the non-exploiting masses of the countryside. This prospect must remain in force for the whole preparatory period, that is, until the victorious revolution in the advanced countries liberates the Soviet Union from its present isolated position.

Some of the thoughts expressed here are developed in greater detail in other works by the author, particularly in the 'Criticism of the Draft Program of the Comintern.' In the near future I hope to publish a pamphlet especially devoted to an evaluation of the present stage of economic development of the USSR. To these works I am obliged to direct the reader who seeks a closer acquaintance with the way in which the problem of the permanent revolution is posed *today*. But the considerations brought out above are sufficient, let me hope, to reveal the full significance of the struggle over principles which was carried on in recent years, and is being carried on right now in the shape of two contrasting theories: *socialism in one country versus the permanent revolution.* Only this topical significance of the question justifies the fact that we present here to foreign readers a book that is largely devoted to a critical reproduction of the pre-revolutionary prognoses and theoretical disputes among the Russian Marxists. A different form of exposition of the questions that interest us might, of course, have been selected. But this form was never created by the author, and was not selected by him of his own accord. It was imposed upon him partly by the opponent's will and partly by the very course of political development. Even the truths of mathematics, the most abstract of the sciences, can best be learned in connection with the history of their discovery. This applies with even greater force to the more concrete, i.e. historically-conditioned truths of Marxist politics. The history of the origin and development of the prognoses of the revolution under the conditions of pre-revolutionary Russia will, I think, bring the reader much closer and far more concretely to the essence of the revolutionary tasks of the world proletariat than a scholastic and pedantic exposition of these political ideas, torn out of the conditions of struggle which gave them birth.

March 29, 1930.

CHAPTER ONE

THE ENFORCED NATURE OF THIS WORK AND ITS AIM

The demand for theory in the party under the leadership of the Right-Centrist bloc has been met for six successive years by anti-Trotskyism, this being the one and only product available in unlimited quantities and for free distribution. Stalin engaged in theory for the first time in 1924, with the immortal articles against the permanent revolution. Even Molotov was baptized as a 'leader' in this font. Falsification is in full swing. A few days ago I happened upon an announcement of the publication in German of Lenin's writings of 1917. This is an invaluable gift to the advanced German working class. One can, however, picture in advance what a lot of falsifications there will be in the text and more especially in the notes. It is enough to point out that first place in the table of contents is given to Lenin's letters to Kollontai in New York. Why? Merely because these letters contain harsh remarks about me, based on *completely false* information from Kollontai, who had given her organic Menshevism an inoculation of hysterical ultra-leftism in those days. In the Russian edition the epigones were compelled to indicate, even if only ambiguously, that Lenin had been misinformed. But it may be assumed that the German edition will not present even this evasive reservation. We might also add that in the same letters of Lenin to Kollontai there are furious assaults upon Bukharin, with whom Kollontai was then in solidarity. This aspect of the letters has been suppressed, however, for the time being. It will be made public only when an open campaign against Bukharin is launched. We shall not have to wait very long for that.[1] On the other hand a number of very valuable documents, articles and speeches of Lenin's, as well as minutes, letters, etc., remain concealed only because they are directed against Stalin and Co. and undermine the legend of 'Trotskyism.' Of the history of the three Russian revolutions, as well as the history of the party, literally not a single shred has been left intact: theory, facts, traditions, the heritage of Lenin, all these have been sacrificed to the struggle against 'Trotskyism,' which was invented and organized, after Lenin was taken ill, as a personal struggle against Trotsky, and which later developed into a struggle against Marxism.

It has again been confirmed that what might appear as the most useless raking up of long-extinct disputes usually satisfies some unconscious social requirement of the day, a requirement which, in itself, does not follow the line of old disputes. The campaign against 'the old Trotskyism' was in a reality a campaign against the October traditions, which had become more and more cramping and unbearable for the new bureaucracy. They began to characterize as 'Trotskyism' everything they wanted to get rid of. Thus the struggle against Trotskyism gradually became the expression of the theoretical and political *reaction* among broad non-proletarian and partly also among proletarian circles, and the reflection of this reaction inside the party. In particular, the caricatured and historically distorted counter-position of the permanent revolution to Lenin's line of 'alliance with the muzhik' sprang full-grown in 1923. It arose along with the period of social, political and party reaction, as its most graphic expression, as the organic antagonism of the bureaucrat and the property-owner to world revolution with its 'permanent' disturbances, and the yearning of the petty-bourgeoisie and officialdom for tranquility and order. The vicious baiting of the permanent revolution served, in turn, only to clear the ground for the theory of socialism in one country, that is, for the latest variety of National Socialism. In themselves, of course, these new social roots of the struggle against 'Trotskyism' do not prove anything either for or against the correctness of the theory of the permanent revolution. Yet, without an understanding of these hidden roots, the controversy must inevitably bear a barren academic character.

In recent years I have not found it possible to tear myself away from the new problems and return to old questions which are bound up with the period of the 1905 Revolution, in so far as these questions are primarily concerned with my past and have been artificially used against it. To give an analysis of the old differences of opinion and particularly of my old mistakes, against the background of the situation in which they arose— an analysis so thorough that these controversies and mistakes would become comprehensible to the young generation, not to speak of the old-timers who have fallen into political second childhood—this would require a whole volume to itself. It seemed monstrous to me to waste my own and others' time upon it, when constantly new questions of enormous importance were being placed on the order of the day: the tasks of the German Revolution, the question of the future fate of Britain, the question of the interrelationship of America and Europe, the problems broached by the strikes of the British proletariat, the tasks of the Chinese Revolution and, lastly and mainly, our own internal economic and socio-political contradictions and tasks—all this, I believe, amply justified my continual putting-off of my historico-polemical work on the permanent revolution. But social consciousness abhors a vacuum. In recent years this theoretical vacuum has been, as I have said, filled up with the rubbish of anti-Trotskyism. The epigones, the philosophers and the brokers of party reaction slipped down ever lower, went to school under the dull-witted Menshevik Martynov, trampled Lenin underfoot, floundered around in the swamp, and called all this the struggle against Trotskyism. In all these years they have not managed to produce a single work serious or important enough to be mentioned out loud without a feeling of shame; they did not bring forth a single political appraisal that has retained its validity, not a single prognosis that has been confirmed, not a single independent slogan that has advanced us ideologically. Nothing but trash and hack-work everywhere.

Stalin's *Problems of Leninism* constitutes a codification of this ideological garbage, an official manual of narrow-mindedness, an anthology of enumerated banalities (I am doing my best to find the most moderate designations possible). *Leninism* by Zinoviev is ... Zinovievist Leninism, and nothing more or less. Zinoviev acts almost on **Luther**'s principle. But whereas Luther said, 'Here I stand; I cannot do otherwise.'

Zinoviev says, 'Here I stand ... but I can do otherwise, too.' To occupy oneself in either case with these theoretical products of epigonism is equally unbearable, with this difference: that in reading Zinoviev's *Leninism* one experiences the sensation of choking on loose cotton-wool, while Stalin's Problems evokes the sensation of finely-chopped bristles. These two books are, each in its own way, the image and crown of the epoch of ideological reaction.

Fitting and adjusting all questions, whether from the right or the left, from above or below, from before or behind—to Trotskyism, the epigones have finally contrived to make every world event directly or indirectly dependent upon how the permanent revolution looked to Trotsky in 1905. The legend of Trotskyism, chock-full of falsifications, has become to a certain extent a factor in contemporary history. And while the right-centrist line of recent years has compromised itself in every continent by bankruptcies of historic dimensions, the struggle against the centrist ideology in the Comintern is today already unthinkable, or at least made very difficult, without an evaluation of the old disputes and prognosis that originated at the beginning of 1905.

The resurrection of Marxist, and consequently Leninist, thought in the party is unthinkable without a polemical auto-da-fe of the scribbling of the epigones, without a merciless theoretical execution of the Party-machine ushers. It is really not difficult to write such a book. All its ingredients are to hand. But it is also hard to write such a book, precisely because in doing so one must, in the words of the great satirist Saltykov, descend into the domain of 'ABC effluvia' and dwell for a considerable time in this scarcely ambrosial atmosphere. Nevertheless, the work has become absolutely unpostponable, for it is precisely upon the struggle against the permanent revolution that the defense of the opportunist line in the problems of the East, that is, the larger half of humanity, is directly constructed.

I was already on the point of entering into this hardly alluring task of theoretical polemic with Zinoviev and Stalin, putting aside our Russian classics for my recreation hours (even divers must rise to the surface now and then to breathe a draught of fresh air) when, quite unexpected by me, an article by Radek appeared and began to circulate, devoted to the 'more profound' counter-position of the theory of the permanent revolution to Lenin's views on this subject. At first I wanted to put

Radek's work aside, lest I be distracted from the combination of loose cotton-wool and finely chopped bristles intended for me by fate. But a number of letters from friends induced me to read Radek's work more attentively, and I came to the following conclusion: for a smaller circle of persons who are capable of thinking independently and not upon command, and are conscientiously studying Marxism, Radek's work is more dangerous than the official literature—just as opportunism in politics is all the more dangerous the more camouflaged it is and the greater the personal reputation that covers it. Radek is one of my closest political friends. This has been amply witnessed by the events of the latest period. In recent months, however, various comrades have followed with misgivings the evolution of Radek, who has moved all the way over from the extreme Left Wing of the Opposition to its Right Wing. All of us who are Radek's intimate friends know that his brilliant political and literary gifts, which are combined with an exceptional impulsiveness and impressionability, are qualities which constitute a valuable source of initiative and criticism under conditions of collective work, but which can produce entirely different fruits under conditions of isolation. Radek's latest work—in connection with a number of his actions preceding it—leads to the opinion that Radek has lost his compass, or that his compass is under the influence of a steady magnetic disturbance. Radek's work is in no sense an episodic excursion into the past. No, it is an insufficiently thought-out but no less harmful contribution in support of the official course, with all its theoretical mythology.

The above-characterized political function of the present struggle against 'Trotskyism' naturally does not in any way signify that within the Opposition, which took shape as the Marxist buttress against the ideological and political reaction, internal criticism is inadmissible, in particular criticism of my old differences of opinion with Lenin. On the contrary such a work of self-clarification could only be fruitful. But here, at all events, a scrupulous preservation of historical perspective, a serious investigation of original sources and an illumination of the past differences in the light of the present struggle, would be absolutely necessary. There is not a trace of all this in Radek. As if unaware of what he is doing, he simply falls into step with the struggle against 'Trotskyism,' utilizing not only the one-sidedly selected quotations, but also the utterly false official interpretations of them. Where he seemingly separates himself from the official campaign, he does it in so ambiguous a manner that he really supplies it with the twofold support of an 'important' witness. As always happens in a case of ideological backsliding, the latest work of Radek does not contain a single trace of his political perspicacity and his literary skill. It is a work without perspective, without depth, a work solely on the plane of quotations, and precisely for this reason—*flat*.

Out of what political needs was it born? Out of the differences of opinion that arose between Radek and the overwhelming majority of the Opposition on the questions of the Chinese Revolution. A few objections are heard, it is true, to the effect that the differences of opinion on China are 'not relevant today' (Preobrazhensky). But these objections do not merit serious consideration. The whole of Bolshevism grew and definitely took shape in the criticism and the assimilation of the experiences of 1905, in all their freshness, while these experiences were still an *immediate experience* of the first generation of Bolsheviks. How could it be otherwise? And what other event could the new generation of proletarian revolutionists learn from today if not from the fresh, still uncongealed experiences of the Chinese Revolution, still reeking with blood? Only lifeless pedants are capable of 'postponing' the questions of the Chinese Revolution, in order to study them later on at leisure and in 'tranquility'. It becomes Bolshevik-Leninists all the less, since the revolutions in the countries of the East have in no sense been removed from the order of the day and their dates are not known to anybody.

Adopting a false position on the problems of the Chinese Revolution, Radek attempts to justify this position retrospectively by a one-sided and distorted presentation of my old differences of opinion with Lenin. And this is where Radek is compelled to borrow weapons from another's arsenal and to navigate without a compass in another's channel.

Radek is my friend, but the truth is dearer to me. I am compelled once again to set aside the more extensive work on the problems of revolution in order to refute Radek. Questions have been raised that are far too important to ignore, and they have been raised point-blank. I have a threefold difficulty to overcome here: the multiplicity and variety of errors in Radek's work; the profusion of literary and historical facts over twenty-three years (1905-28) that refute Radek; and thirdly, the short time that I can devote to this work, for the economic problems of the USSR are pressing to the foreground.

All these circumstances determine the character of the present work. This work does not exhaust the question. There is much that remains unsaid—in part, incidentally, because it is a sequel to other works, primarily the *Criticism of the Draft Programme of the Communist International*. Mountains of factual material which I have assembled on this question must remain unused—pending the writing of my contemplated book against the epigones, that is, against the official ideology of the era of reaction.

Radek's work on the permanent revolution rests on the conclusion:

'The new section of the party (The Opposition) is threatened with the danger of the rise of tendencies which will tear the development of the proletarian revolution away from its ally—the peasantry.'

One is first of all astonished by the fact that this conclusion concerning a 'new' section of the party is adduced during the second half of the year 1928 as a new conclusion. We have already heard it reiterated constantly since the autumn of 1923. But how does Radek justify his going-over to the main official thesis? Again, not in a new way: He turns back to the theory of the permanent revolution. In 1924-25, Radek more than once intended to write a pamphlet dedicated to proving the idea that the theory of the permanent revolution and Lenin's slogan of the democratic dictatorship of the proletariat and peasantry, taken on an historical scale—that is, in the light of the experience of our three revolutions—could in no case be counter-posed to each other but were, on the contrary, essentially the same. Now, after having thoroughly examined the question 'anew'— as he writes to one of his friends—Radek has reached the conclusion that the old theory of the permanent revolution threatens the 'new' section of the party with nothing more or less than the danger of a breach with the peasantry.

But how did Radek 'thoroughly examine' this question? He gives us some information on this point:

We do not have at hand the formulations which Trotsky presented in 1904 in a preface to Marx's *Civil War in France* and in 1905 in *Our Revolution*.

The years are not correctly stated here, but it is not worthwhile to dwell upon this. The whole point is that the only work in which I presented my views more or less systematically on the development of the revolution is a rather extensive article, *Results and Prospects* (in *Our Revolution*, Petersburg, 1906, pages 224-86). The article in the Polish organ of Rosa Luxemburg and Tyszko (1909), to which Radek refers, but unfortunately interprets in Kamenev's way, lays no claim to completeness or comprehensiveness. Theoretically this work is based upon the above-mentioned book *Our Revolution*. Nobody is obliged to read this book now. Since that time such great events have taken place and we have learned so much from these events that, to tell the truth, I feel an aversion to the epigones' present manner of considering new historical problems not in the light of the living experience of the revolutions already carried out by us, but mainly in the light of quotations that relate only to our forecasts regarding what were then *future* revolutions. Naturally, by this I do not want to deprive Radek of the right to take up the question from the historico-literary side also. But in that case, it must be done properly. Radek undertakes to illuminate the fate of the theory of the permanent revolution in the course of almost a quarter of a century, and remarks in passing that he 'has not at hand' precisely those documents in which I set down this theory.

I want to point out right here that Lenin, as has become particularly clear to me now in reading his old articles, never read my basic work mentioned above. This is probably to be explained not only by the fact that *Our Revolution*, which appeared in 1906, was soon confiscated and that all of us shortly went into emigration, but also perhaps by the fact that two-thirds of the book consisted of reprints of old articles. I heard later from many comrades that they had not read this book because they thought it consisted exclusively of reprints of old works. In any case, the few scattered polemical remarks of Lenin against the permanent revolution are based almost exclusively upon the foreword by Parvus to my pamphlet *Before the Ninth of January*; upon Parvus's Proclamation No Tsar! which remained completely unknown to me; and upon internal disputes of Lenin's with Bukharin and others. Never did Lenin anywhere analyze or quote, even in passing, *Results and Prospects*, and certain objections of Lenin to the permanent revolution, which obviously have no reference to me, directly prove that he did not read this work.[2]

It would be rash to suppose, however, that this is just what Lenin's 'Leninism' consists of. But this seems to be Radek's opinion. In any case, Radek's article which I have to examine here shows not only that he did 'not have at hand' my fundamental works, but also that he had never even read them. If he did, then it was long ago, before the October Revolution. In any case he did not retain much of it in his memory.

But the matter does not end there. It was admissible and even unavoidable in 1905 or 1909 to polemicize with each other over individual articles that were topical then and even over single sentences in isolated articles—especially under the conditions of the split. But today it is impermissible for a revolutionary Marxist, should he want to review retrospectively this tremendous historical period, not to ask himself the question: How were the formulas under discussion applied in practice? How were they interpreted and construed in action? What tactics were applied? Had Radek taken the trouble to glance through merely the two books of *Our First Revolution* (volume II of my *Collected Works*), he would not have ventured to write his present work; at all events, he would have struck out a whole series of his sweeping contentions. At least, I should like to hope he would.

From these two books Radek would have learned, in the first place, that in my political activity the permanent revolution in no case signified for me a jumping-over of the democratic stage of the revolution or any of its specific steps. He would have convinced himself that, though I lived in Russia illegally throughout 1905 without any connection with the emigrants, I formulated the tasks of the successive stages of the revolution in exactly the same manner as Lenin; he would have learned that the fundamental appeals to the peasants that were issued by the central press of the Bolsheviks in 1905 were written by me; that the *Novaya Zhizn (New Life)*, edited by Lenin, in an editorial note resolutely defended my article on the permanent revolution which appeared in *Nachalo (The Beginning)*; that Lenin's *Novaya Zhizn*, and on occasion Lenin personally, supported and defended invariably those political decisions of the Soviets of Deputies which were written by me and on which I acted as reporter nine times out of ten; that, after the December defeat, I wrote while in prison a pamphlet on tactics in which I pointed out that the combination of the proletarian offensive with the agrarian revolution of the peasants was the central strategic problem; that Lenin had this pamphlet published by the Bolshevik publishing house *Novaya Volna (New Wave)* and informed me through Knunyants of his hearty approval; that Lenin spoke at the London Congress in 1907 of my 'solidarity' with Bolshevism in my views on the peasantry and the liberal bourgeoisie. None of this exists for Radek; evidently he did not have this 'at hand' either.

How does the matter stand with Radek in relation to the works of Lenin? No better, or not much better. Radek confines himself to those quotations which Lenin did direct against me but quite often intended for others (for example, Bukharin and Radek; an open reference to this is found in Radek himself). Radek was unable to adduce a single new quotation against me; he simply made use of the ready-made quotation material that almost every citizen of the USSR has 'at hand' nowadays. Radek only added a few quotations in which Lenin elucidated elementary truths to the anarchists and Socialist-Revolutionaries on the difference between a bourgeois republic and socialism—and thereupon Radek depicts matters as if these quotations too had been directed against me. Hardly credible, but it is true!

Radek entirely avoids those old declarations in which Lenin, very cautiously and very sparingly but with all the greater weight, recognized my solidarity with Bolshevism on the basic questions of the revolution. Here it must not be forgotten for an instant that Lenin did this at a time when I did not belong to the Bolshevik faction and when Lenin was attacking me mercilessly (and quite rightly so) for my conciliationism—not for the permanent revolution, where he confined himself to occasional objections, but for my conciliationism, for my readiness to hope for an evolution of the Mensheviks to the left. Lenin was much more concerned with the struggle against conciliationism than with the 'justice' of isolated polemical blows against the 'conciliator' Trotsky.

In 1924, defending against me Zinoviev's conduct in October, 1917. Stalin wrote:

Comrade Trotsky fails to understand Lenin's letters (on Zinoviev—L.T.), their significance and their purpose. Lenin sometimes deliberately ran ahead, pushing into the forefront mistakes that might possibly be committed, and criticizing them in advance with the object of warning the party and of safeguarding it against mistakes. Sometimes he would even magnify a "trifle" and "make a mountain out of a molehill" for the same pedagogical purpose.... But to infer from such letters of Lenin's (and he wrote quite a number of such letters) the existence of "tragic" disagreements and to trumpet them forth means not to understand Lenin's letters, means not to know Lenin.' (J. Stalin, *Trotskyism or Leninism*, 1924).

The idea is here formulated crudely—'the style is the man'—but the essence of the idea is correct, even though it applies least of all to the disputes during the October period, which bore no resemblance to 'molehills.' But if Lenin used to resort to 'pedagogical' exaggerations and preventive polemics in relation to the closest members of his own faction, then he did so all the more in relation to an individual who was at the time outside the Bolshevik faction and preached conciliationism. It never occurred to Radek to introduce this necessary corrective coefficient into the old quotations.

In the 1922 foreword of my book *The Year 1905*, I wrote that my forecast of the possibility and probability of establishing the dictatorship of the proletariat in Russia before it was achieved in the advanced countries was verified in reality 12 years later. Radek, following not very attractive examples, represents matters as though I had *counter-posed* this prognosis to Lenin's strategic line. From the foreword, however, it can be clearly seen that I dealt with the prognosis of the permanent revolution from the standpoint of those basic features which *coincide* with the *strategic* line of Bolshevism. When I speak in a footnote of the 'rearming' of the party at the beginning of 1917, then it is certainly not in the sense that Lenin recognized the previous road of the party as 'erroneous' but rather that Lenin came to Russia—even though delayed, yet opportunely enough for the success of the revolution—to teach the party to *reject the outlived slogan* of the 'democratic dictatorship' to which the Stalins, Kamenevs, Rykovs,

Molotovs and others were still clinging. When the Kamenevs grow indignant at the mention of the 'rearming,' this is comprehensible, for it was undertaken against them. But Radek? He first began to grow indignant only in 1928, that is, only after he himself had begun to fight against the necessary 'rearming' of the Chinese Communist Party.

Let me remind Radek that my books *The Year 1905* (with the criminal foreword) and *The October Revolution* played the role, while Lenin was alive, of fundamental historical textbooks on both revolutions. At that time, they went through innumerable editions in Russian as well as in foreign languages. Never did anybody tell me that my books contained a counter-posing of two lines, because at that time, before the revisionist volte-face by the epigones, no sound-thinking party member subordinated the October experience to old quotations, but instead viewed old quotations in the light of the October Revolution.

In connection with this there is one other subject which Radek misuses in an impermissible manner: Trotsky did acknowledge—he says—that Lenin was right against him. Of course I did. And in this acknowledgment there was not one iota of diplomacy. I had in mind the whole historical road of Lenin, his whole theoretical position, his strategy, his building of the party. This acknowledgment certainly does not, however, apply to every single one of the polemical quotations—which are, moreover, misused today for purposes hostile to Leninism. In 1926, in the period of the bloc with Zinoviev, Radek warned me that Zinoviev needed my declaration that Lenin was right, as against me, in order to screen somewhat the fact that he, Zinoviev, was wrong as against me. Naturally, I understood this very well. And that is why I said at the Seventh Plenum of the Executive Committee of the Communist International that I meant the historical rightness of Lenin and his party, but in no case the rightness of my present critics, who strive to cover themselves with quotations plucked from Lenin. Today I am unfortunately compelled to extend these words to Radek.

With regard to the permanent revolution, I spoke only of the *defects* of the theory, which were inevitable insofar as it was a question of *prediction*. At the Seventh Plenum of the E.C.C.I., Bukharin rightly emphasized that Trotsky did not renounce the conception as a whole. On the 'defects' I shall speak in another, more extensive work, in which I shall endeavor to present the experiences of the three revolutions and their application to the further course of the Comintern, especially in the East. But in order to leave no room for misunderstandings, I wish to say here briefly: Despite all its defects, the theory of the permanent revolution, even as presented in my earliest works, primarily *Results and Prospects* (1906), is immeasurably more permeated with the spirit of Marxism and consequently far closer to the historical line of Lenin and the Bolshevik Party, than not only the present Stalinist and Bukharinist retrospective wisdom but also the latest work of Radek.

By this I do not at all want to say that my conception of the revolution follows, in all my writings, one and the same unswerving line. I did not occupy myself with collecting old quotations—I am forced to do so now only by the period of party reaction and epigonism—but I tried, for better or for worse, to analyze the real processes of life. In the 12 years (1905-17) of my revolutionary journalistic activity, there are also articles in which the episodic circumstances and even the episodic polemical exaggerations inevitable in struggle protrude into the foreground in violation of the strategic line. Thus, for example, articles can be found in which I expressed doubts about the future revolutionary role of the peasantry *as a whole, as an estate*, and in connection with this refused to designate, especially during the imperialist war, the future Russian revolution as 'national,' for I felt this designation to be ambiguous. But it must not be forgotten here that the historical processes that interest us, including the processes in the peasantry, are far more obvious now that they have been accomplished than they were in those days when they were only developing. Let me also remark that Lenin—who never for a moment lost sight of the peasant question in all its gigantic historical magnitude and from whom we all learned this—considered it uncertain even after the February Revolution whether we should succeed in tearing the peasantry away from the bourgeoisie and drawing it after the proletariat. I will say quite in general to my harsh critics that it is far easier to dig out in one hour the formal contradictions of another person's newspaper articles over a quarter of a century, than it is to preserve, oneself, if only for a year, unity of fundamental line.

There remains only to mention in these introductory lines one other completely ritualistic consideration: had the theory of the permanent revolution been incorrect—says Radek—Trotsky would have assembled a large faction on that basis. But that did not happen. Therefore it follows... that the theory was false.

This argument of Radek's, *taken as a general proposition*, does not contain a trace of dialectics. One could conclude from it that the standpoint of the Opposition on the Chinese Revolution or the position of Marx on British affairs was false; that the position of the Comintern with regard to the reformists in America, in Austria and—if you wish—in all countries, is false.

If Radek's argument is taken not in its general 'historico-philosophical' form, but only as applied to the question under discussion, then it hits Radek himself. The argument might have a shade of sense had I been of the opinion or, what is still more important, had events shown, that the line of the permanent revolution *contradicts* the strategic line of Bolshevism, *stands in conflict* with it, and *diverges* from it more and more. Only then would there have been grounds for two factions. But that is just what Radek wants to prove. I show, on the contrary, that in spite of all the factional polemical exaggerations and conjectural accentuations of the question, the basic strategic line was one and the same. Where, then, should a second faction have come from? In reality, it turned out that I worked hand in hand with the Bolsheviks in the first revolution and later defended this joint work in the international press against the Menshevik renegades' criticism. In the 1917 Revolution I fought together with Lenin against the democratic opportunism of those 'old Bolsheviks' who have today been elevated by the reactionary wave and whose sole armament consists of their baiting of the permanent revolution.

Finally, I never endeavored to create a grouping on the basis of the ideas of the permanent revolution. My inner-party stand was a *conciliationist* one, and when at certain moments I strove for the formation of groupings, then it was precisely on this basis. My conciliationism flowed from a sort of social-revolutionary fatalism. I believed that the logic of the class struggle would compel both factions to pursue the same revolutionary line. The great historical significance of Lenin's policy was still unclear to me at that time, his policy of irreconcilable ideological demarcation and, when necessary, split, for the purpose of welding and tempering the core of the truly revolutionary party. In 1911, Lenin wrote on this subject:

Conciliationism is the sum total of moods, strivings and views which are indissolubly bound up with the very essence of the historical task set before the Russian Social Democratic Party during the period of the counter-revolution of 1908-11. That is why, during that period, a number of Social Democrats, *starting from quite different premises*, fell into conciliationism. Trotsky expressed conciliationism more consistently than anyone else. He was probably the only one who attempted to give this tendency a theoretical foundation.

By striving for unity at all costs, I involuntarily and unavoidably idealized centrist tendencies in Menshevik Menshevism. Despite my thrice-repeated episodic attempts, I arrived at no common task with the Mensheviks, and I could not arrive at it. Simultaneously, however, the conciliationist line brought me into still sharper conflict with Bolshevism, since Lenin, in contrast to the Mensheviks, relentlessly rejected conciliationism, and could not but do this. It is obvious that no faction could be created on the platform of conciliationism.

Hence the lesson: It is impermissible and fatal to break or weaken a political line for purposes of vulgar conciliationism; it is impermissible to paint up centrism when it zig-zags to the left; it is impermissible, in the hunt after the will-o'-the-wisps of centrism, to exaggerate and inflate differences of opinion with genuine revolutionary co-thinkers. These are the real lessons of Trotsky's real mistakes. These lessons are very important. They preserve their full force even today, and it is precisely Radek who should meditate upon them.

With the ideological cynicism characteristic of him, Stalin once said :

Trotsky cannot but know that Lenin fought against the theory of the permanent revolution to the end of his life. But that does not worry Trotsky.

This is a crude and disloyal, that is, a purely Stalinist caricature of the reality. In one of his communications to foreign Communists, Lenin explained that differences of opinion among Communists are something quite different from differences of opinion with the Social Democrats. Such differences of opinion, he wrote, **Bolshevism** had also gone through in the past. But '... at the moment when it seized power and created the Soviet Republic, Bolshevism proved united and *drew to itself all the best of the currents of socialist thought that were nearest to it. . . .'*

What nearest currents of socialist thought did Lenin have in mind when he wrote these lines? Martynov or Kuusinen? Or Cachin, Thaelmann and Smeral? Did they perhaps appear to him as the 'best of the nearest currents'? What other tendency was nearer to Bolshevism than the one which I represented on all fundamental questions, including the peasant question? Even Rosa Luxemburg shrank back at first from the agrarian policy of the Bolshevik government. For me, however, there was no doubt about this at all. I was together with Lenin at the table when, pencil in hand, he drafted his agrarian law. And our interchange of opinions hardly consisted of more than a dozen brief remarks, the sense of which was about the following: The step is a contradictory one, but historically it is absolutely unavoidable; under the regime of the proletarian dictatorship and on the scale of world revolution, the contradictions will be adjusted—we only need time. If a basic antagonism existed on the peasant question between the theory of the permanent revolution and Lenin's dialectic how then does Radek explain the fact that without renouncing my basic views on the course of development of the revolution, I did not stumble in the slightest over the peasant question in 1917, as did the majority of the Bolshevik leadership of that time? How does Radek explain the fact that after the February Revolution the present theoreticians and politicians of anti-Trotskyism—Zinoviev, Kamenev, Stalin, Rykov, Molotov, etc., etc.—adopted, to the last man, the vulgar-democratic and not the proletarian position? And once again: Of what and of whom could Lenin have spoken when he referred to the merging of Bolshevism and the best elements of the Marxist currents nearest to it? And does not this evaluation in which Lenin *drew the balance sheet* of the past differences of opinion show that in any case he saw no two irreconcilable strategic lines?

Still more noteworthy in this respect is Lenin's speech at the November 1 (14), 1917, session of the Petrograd Committee.[3] There the question was discussed, whether to make an agreement with the Mensheviks and the Socialist-Revolutionaries. The supporters of a coalition endeavored even there—very timidly, to be sure—to hint at 'Trotskyism'. What did Lenin reply?

Agreement? I cannot even speak seriously about that. Trotsky has long ago said that unity is impossible. Trotsky understood this—and since then there has been no better Bolshevik.

Not the permanent revolution but conciliationism was what separated me, in Lenin's opinion, from Bolshevism. In order to become the 'best Bolshevik', I only needed, as we see, to understand the impossibility of an agreement with Menshevism.

But how is the abrupt character of Radek's turn precisely on the question of the permanent revolution to be explained? I believe I have one element of explanation. In 1916, as we learn from his article, Radek was in agreement with 'permanent revolution'; but his agreement was with Bukharin's interpretation of it, according to which the bourgeois revolution in Russia had been completed—not only the revolutionary role of the bourgeoisie, and not even only the historical role of the slogan of the democratic dictatorship, but the bourgeois revolution as such—and the proletariat must therefore proceed to the capture of power under a purely socialist banner. Radek manifestly interpreted my position at that time also in the Bukharinist manner; otherwise he could not have declared his solidarity with Bukharin and me at one and the same time. This also explains why Lenin polemized against Bukharin and Radek, with whom he collaborated, having them appears under the pseudonym of Trotsky. (Radek admits this also in his article.) I remember also that M. N. Pokrovsky, a co-thinker of Bukharin's and a tireless constructor of historical schemas which he very skillfully painted up as Marxism, alarmed me in conversations I had with him in Paris with his dubious 'solidarity' on this question. In politics, Pokrovsky was and remains an anti-Cadet, which he honestly believes to constitute Bolshevism.

In 1924-25, Radek apparently still lived upon ideological recollections of the Bukharinist position of 1916, which he continued to identify with mine. Rightly disillusioned with this hopeless position, Radek—on the basis of a fleeting study of Lenin's writings—as frequently happens in such cases, described an arc of 180 degrees right over my head. This is quite probable, because it is typical. Thus, Bukharin, who in 1923-25 turned himself inside out, that is, transformed himself from an ultra-left into an opportunist, constantly attributes to me his own ideological past, which he palms off as 'Trotskyism'. In the first period of the campaign against me, when I still forced myself occasionally to read Bukharin's articles, I would frequently ask myself: Where did he get this from?— but I soon guessed that he had glanced into his diary of yesterday. And now I wonder if the same psychological foundation does not lie at the bottom of Radek's conversion from a Paul of the permanent revolution into its Saul. I do not presume to insist upon this hypothesis. But I can find no other explanation.

Anyway, as the French saying goes: the wine is drawn, it must be drunk. We are compelled to undertake a lengthy excursion into the realm of old quotations. I have reduced their number as much as was feasible. Yet there are still many of them. Let it serve as my justification, that I strive throughout to find in my enforced rummaging among these old quotations the threads that connect up with the burning questions of the present time.

Notes

1. This prediction has in the meantime been fulfilled.—L.T.

2. In 1909 Lenin did indeed quote my *Results and Prospects* in an article polemicizing against Martov. It would not, however, be difficult to prove that Lenin took over the quotations at second-hand, that is, from Martov himself. This is the only way that certain of his objections directed at me, which are based upon obvious misunderstandings, can be explained. In 1919, the State Publishing House issued my *Results and Prospects* as a pamphlet. The annotation to the complete edition of Lenin's works, to the effect that the theory of the permanent revolution is especially noteworthy 'now', after the [[Wikipedia:October Revolution, dates back to approximately the same time. Did Lenin read my *Results and Prospects* in 1919 or merely glance through it? On this I cannot say anything definite. I was then constantly traveling, came to Moscow only for short stays, and during my meetings with Lenin in that period—at the height of the civil war—factional theoretical reminiscences never entered our minds. But A. A. Joffe did have a conversation with Lenin, just at that time, on the theory of the permanent revolution. Joffe reported this conversation

in the farewell letter he wrote me before his death. (See *My Life*, New York, pages 535, 537.) Can A. A. Joffe's assertions be construed meaning that Lenin in 1919 became acquainted *for the first time with Results and Prospects* and recognized the correctness of the historical prognosis contained in it? On this matter I can only express psychological conjectures. The power of conviction of these conjectures depends upon the evaluation of the kernel of the disputed question itself. A. A. Joffe's words, that Lenin had confirmed my prognosis as correct, must appear incomprehensible to a man who has been raised upon the theoretical margarine of the post-Leninist epoch. On the other hand, whoever reflects upon the evolution of Lenin's ideas in connection with the development of the revolution itself will understand that Lenin, in 1919 had to make—could not have failed to make—a new evaluation of the theory of the permanent revolution, different from the ones he had pronounced desultorily, in passing, and often manifestly self-contradictory, at various times before the October Revolution, on the basis of isolated quotations, without even once examining my position as a whole.

In order to confirm my prognosis as correct in 1919, Lenin did not need to counter-pose my position to his. It sufficed to consider both positions in their historical development. It is not necessary to repeat here that the concrete content which Lenin always gave to his formula of 'democratic dictatorship', and which flowed less from a hypothetical formula than from the analysis of the actual changes in class relationships—that this tactical and organizational content has passed once and for all into the inventory of history as a classic model of revolutionary realism. In almost all the cases, at any rate in all the most important cases, where I placed myself in contradiction to Lenin tactically or organizationally, right was on his side. That is just why it did not interest me to come forward in favor of my old historical prognosis, so long as it might appear that it was only a matter of historical reminiscences. I found myself compelled to return to this question only at the moment when the epigones criticism of the theory of the permanent revolution not only began to nurture theoretical reaction in the whole International, but also became converted into a means of direct sabotage of the Chinese Revolution.—L.T.

3. As is known, the voluminous minutes of this historic session were torn out of the *Jubilee Book* by special command of Stalin and to this day are kept concealed from the party.—L.T.

CHAPTER TWO

THE PERMANENT REVOLUTION IS NOT A 'LEAP' BY THE PROLETARIAT. BUT THE RECONSTRUCTION OF THE NATION UNDER THE LEADERSHIP OF THE PROLETARIAT

Radek writes:

The essential feature that distinguishes the train of thought which is called the theory and tactic (observe: tactic, too.—L.T.) of the "permanent revolution" from Lenin's theory lies in *mixing up the stage of the bourgeois revolution with the stage of the socialist revolution.*

Connected with this fundamental accusation, or resulting from it, there are other no less serious accusations: Trotsky did not understand that 'under Russian conditions, a socialist revolution which does not grow out of the democratic revolution is impossible'; and from this followed 'skipping the stage of the democratic dictatorship'. Trotsky 'denied' the role of the peasantry, which is where 'the community of views of Trotsky and the Mensheviks' lay. As already said, all this is intended to prove, by means of circumstantial evidence, the incorrectness of my position on the fundamental questions of the Chinese Revolution.

To be sure, so far as the formal literary side is concerned, Radek can refer here and there to Lenin. And he does that; everybody has 'at hand' *this* section of the quotations. But as I shall presently demonstrate, these contentions of Lenin in regard to me had a purely episodic character and were incorrect, that is, in no sense did they characterize what my real position was, even in 1905. In Lenin's own writings there are quite different, directly contrary and far better grounded remarks on my attitude on the basic questions of the revolution. Radek did not even make the attempt to unite the various and directly contradictory remarks of Lenin, and to elucidate these polemical contradictions by a comparison with my actual views.[1]

In 1906, Lenin published, with his own foreword, an article by Kautsky on the driving forces of the Russian Revolution. Without knowing anything about this, I also translated Kautsky's article in prison, provided it with a foreword and included it in my book *In Defence of the Party*. Both Lenin and I expressed our thorough accord with Kautsky's analysis. To Plekhanov's question: Is our revolution bourgeois or socialist? Kautsky had answered that it is no longer bourgeois, but not yet socialist, that is, it represents the transitional form from the one to the other. In this connection, Lenin wrote in his foreword:

Is our revolution bourgeois or socialist in its general character? That is the old schema, says Kautsky. That is not how the question should be put, that is not the Marxist way. The revolution in Russia is not bourgeois, for the bourgeoisie is not one of the driving forces of the present revolutionary movement in Russia. But neither is the revolution in Russia socialist.

Yet not a few passages can be found in Lenin, written both before and after this foreword, where he categorically calls the Russian Revolution bourgeois. Is this a contradiction? If Lenin is approached with the methods of the present critics of 'Trotskyism', then dozens and hundreds of such contradictions can be found without difficulty, which are clarified for the serious and conscientious reader by the difference in the approach to the question at different times, which in no way violates the fundamental unity of Lenin's conception.

On the other hand, I never denied the *bourgeois* character of the revolution in the sense of its immediate historical tasks, but only in the sense of its driving forces and its perspectives. My fundamental work of those days (1905-06) on the permanent revolution begins with the following sentences:

The Russian Revolution came unexpectedly to everybody but the Social Democrats. Marxism long ago predicted the inevitability of the Russian Revolution, which was bound to break out as a result of the conflict between capitalist development and the forces of ossified absolutism ... In calling it a bourgeois revolution, Marxism thereby pointed out that the *immediate objective* tasks of the revolution consisted in the creation of "normal conditions for the development of bourgeois society as a whole". Marxism has proved to be right, and this is now past the need for discussion or proof. The Marxists are now confronted by a task of quite another kind: to discover the "possibilities" of the developing revolution by means of an analysis of its internal mechanism ... The Russian Revolution has a quite peculiar character, which is the result of the peculiar trend of our whole social and historical development, and which in its turn opens before us quite new historical prospects. 'The general sociological term *bourgeois revolution* by no means solves the politico-tactical problems, contradictions and difficulties which the mechanics of a given bourgeois revolution throw up.'

Thus I did not deny the bourgeois character of the revolution that stood on the order of the day, and I did not mix up democracy and socialism. But I endeavored to show that in our country the class dialectics of the bourgeois revolution would bring the proletariat to power and that without its dictatorship not even democratic tasks could be solved.

In the same article (1905-06) I wrote:

The proletariat grows and becomes stronger with the growth of capitalism. In this sense, the development of capitalism is also the development of the proletariat toward dictatorship. But the day and the hour when power will pass into the hands of the working class depends *directly* not upon the level attained by the productive forces but upon the relations in the class struggle, upon the international situation and finally, upon a number of subjective factors: the traditions, the initiative, readiness to fight of the workers.

'It is possible for the workers to come to power in an economically backward country sooner than in an advanced country ... To imagine that the dictatorship of the proletariat is in some way dependent upon the technical development and resources of a country is a prejudice of "economic" materialism simplified to absurdity. This point of view has nothing in common with Marxism.

'In our view, the Russian Revolution will create conditions in which power can pass into the hands of the workers—and in the event of the victory of the revolution it must do so —*before* the politicians of bourgeois liberalism get the chance to display to the full their ability to govern.'

These lines contain a polemic against the vulgar 'Marxism' which not only prevailed in 1905-06, but also set the tone of the March, 1917, conference of the Bolsheviks before Lenin's arrival, and found its crassest expression in Rykov's speech at the April conference. At the Sixth Congress of the Comintern, this pseudo-Marxism, that is, philistine 'common sense' debauched by scholasticism, constituted the 'scientific' basis of the speeches of Kuusinen and many, many others. And this, ten years after the October Revolution!

Since I have not the possibility of setting out here the whole train of thought of 'Results and Prospects', I should like to adduce one more summary quotation from my article in *Nachalo* (1905):

Our liberal bourgeoisie comes forward as a counter-revolutionary force even before the revolutionary climax. At each critical moment, our intellectual democrats only demonstrate their impotence. The peasantry as a whole represents an elemental force in rebellion. It can be put at the service of the revolution only by a force that takes state power into its hands. The vanguard position of the working class in the revolution, the direct connection established between it and the revolutionary countryside, the attraction by which it brings the army under its influence—all this impels it inevitably to power. The complete victory of the revolution means the victory of the proletariat. This in turn means the further uninterrupted character of the revolution.

The prospect of the dictatorship of the proletariat consequently grows here precisely out of the bourgeois-democratic revolution—in contradiction to all that Radek writes. That is just why the revolution is called permanent (uninterrupted). But the dictatorship of the proletariat does not come *after* the completion of the democratic revolution, as Radek would have it. If that were the case it would simply be impossible in Russia, for in a backward country the numerically weak proletariat could not attain power if the tasks of the peasantry had been solved during the preceding stage. No, the dictatorship of the proletariat appeared probable and even inevitable on the basis of the bourgeois revolution precisely because there was no other power and no other way to solve the tasks of the agrarian revolution. But exactly this opens up the prospect of a democratic revolution growing over into the socialist revolution.

'The very fact of the proletariat's representatives entering the government, not as powerless hostages, but as the leading force, destroys the border line between maximum and minimum program; that is to say, it *places collectivism on the order of the day*. The point at which the proletariat will be held up in its advance in this direction depends upon the relation of forces, but in no way upon the original intentions of the proletarian party.

'For this reason there can be no talk of any sort of *special* form of proletarian dictatorship in the bourgeois revolution, of *democratic* proletarian dictatorship (or dictatorship of proletariat and peasantry). The working class cannot preserve the democratic character of its dictatorship without overstepping the limits of its democratic program... 'The proletariat, once having taken power, will fight for it to the very end. While one of the weapons in this struggle for the maintenance and the consolidation of power will be agitation and organization, especially in the countryside, another will be a policy of collectivism. Collectivism will become not only the inevitable way forward from the position in which the party in power will find itself, but will also be a means of preserving this position with the support of the proletariat.'

Let us go further:

'We know a classic example (I wrote in 1908 against the Menshevik Cherevanin) of a revolution in which the conditions for the rule of the capitalist bourgeoisie were prepared by the terrorist dictatorship of the victorious sans-culottes. That was in an epoch when the bulk of the urban population was composed of petty-bourgeoisie of the artisan and tradesman type. It followed the leadership of the Jacobins. The bulk of the urban population in Russia is composed today of the industrial proletariat. This analogy alone points to the possibility of a historical situation in which the victory of the "bourgeois" revolution will prove possible only through the conquest of revolutionary power by the proletariat. Does the revolution thereby cease to be bourgeois? Yes and no. This does not depend upon the formal designation but upon the further development of events. If the proletariat is overthrown by a coalition of bourgeois classes, among them also the peasantry it has liberated, then the revolution will retain its limited bourgeois character. Should the proletariat, however, prove able and find it possible to set in motion all the means of its political rule in order to break through the national framework of the Russian revolution, then the latter can become the prologue to the world socialist cataclysm. The question: what stage will the Russian Revolution attain? permits naturally only a conditional reply. Only one thing is absolutely and indubitably correct: the mere characterization of the Russian revolution as bourgeois tells us nothing about the type of its internal development and in no case signifies that the proletariat must adapt its tactics to the conduct of bourgeois democracy as the sole legal claimant to state power.'

From the same article:

'Our revolution, which is a bourgeois revolution with regard to the immediate tasks it grew out of, knows, as a consequence of the extreme class differentiation of the industrial population, of no bourgeois class capable of placing itself at the head of the popular masses by combining its own social weight and political experience with their revolutionary energy. The oppressed worker and peasant masses, left to their own resources, must take it upon themselves to create, in the hard school of implacable conflicts and cruel defeats, the necessary political and organizational preconditions for their triumph. No other road is open to them.'

One more quotation from *Results and Prospects* must be adduced on the most violently assailed point—on the peasantry. In a special chapter, 'The Proletariat in Power and the Peasantry', the following is said:

'The proletariat, in order to consolidate its power, cannot but widen the base of the revolution. Many sections of the working masses, particularly in the countryside, will be drawn into the revolution and become politically organized only after the advance-guard of the revolution, the urban proletariat, stands at the helm of state. Revolutionary agitation and organization will then be conducted with the help of state resources. The legislative power itself will become a powerful instrument for revolutionizing the masses ...

'The fate of the most elementary revolutionary interests of the peasantry—even the peasantry as a whole, as an *estate*, is bound up with the fate of the revolution, i.e., with the fate of the proletariat. *The proletariat in power will stand before tire peasantry as the class which has emancipated it.* The domination of the proletariat will mean not only democratic equality, free self-government, the transference of the whole burden of taxation to the rich classes, the dissolution of the standing army in the armed people, and the abolition of compulsory church imposts, but also recognition of all revolutionary changes (expropriations) in land relationships carried out by the peasants. The proletariat will make these changes the starting point for further state measures in agriculture. Under such conditions, the Russian peasantry in the first and most difficult period of the revolution, will be interested in the maintenance of a proletarian regime ("workers' democracy") at all events not less than was the French peasantry in the maintenance of the military regime of Napoleon Bonaparte, which guaranteed to the new property owners, by the force of its bayonets, the inviolability of their holdings ...

'But is it not possible that the peasantry may push the proletariat aside and take its place? This is impossible. All historical experience protests against this assumption. Historical experience shows that the peasantry is absolutely incapable of taking up an *independent* political role.'

All this was written not in 1929, nor yet in 1924, but in 1905. Does this look like 'ignoring the peasantry', I should like to know? Where is the 'jumping over' of the agrarian question here? Is it not time, friends, to be somewhat more scrupulous?

Now let us see how 'scrupulous' Stalin is on this question. Referring to my New York articles on the February, 1917, Revolution, which agree in every essential with Lenin's Geneva articles, this theoretician of party reaction writes:

'... Trotsky's letters "do not in the least resemble" Lenin's letters either in spirit or in conclusions, for they wholly and entirely reflect Trotsky's anti-Bolshevik slogan of "no Tsar, but a workers' government", a slogan which implies a revolution *without* the peasantry.' (Speech to the

Party fraction in the All-Union Central Committee of the Trade Unions, November 19, 1924.)

Remarkable is the sound of these words on the 'anti-Bolshevik slogan' (allegedly Trotsky's): 'No Tsar—but a workers' government.' According to Stalin, the Bolshevik slogan should have read: 'No workers' government, but a Tsar.' We will speak later of this alleged 'slogan' of Trotsky's. But first let us hear from another would-be master of contemporary thought, less illiterate perhaps, but one who has taken leave forever of any theoretical scruples—I speak of Lunacharsky:

'In 1905, Lev Davidovich Trotsky inclined to the idea: *the proletariat must remain isolated* (!) and must not support the bourgeoisie, for that would be opportunism; for the proletariat alone, however, it would be very difficult to carry through the revolution, because the proletariat at that time amounted to only seven to eight per cent of the total population and victory could not be won with so small a cadre. Thus, Lev Davidovich decided that the proletariat must maintain a permanent revolution in Russia that is, fight for the greatest possible results until the fiery sparks of this conflagration should blow up the entire world powder-magazine.'

The proletariat 'must remain isolated' until the fiery sparks blow up the powder magazines ...How well many People's Commissars write who are for the moment not yet 'isolated' in spite of the threatened position of their own little heads. But we do not want to be too hard on Lunacharsky; from each according to his abilities. In the last analysis, his slovenly absurdities are no more senseless than those of many others.

But how, according to Trotsky, must 'the proletariat remain isolated' ? Let us adduce one quotation from my pamphlet against Struve (1906). At that time, by the way, Lunarcharsky praised this work immoderately. In the chapter that deals with the Soviet of Deputies, it is stated that while the bourgeois parties 'remained completely on the sidelines', away from the awakening masses, 'political life became concentrated around the workers' **Soviet**. The attitude of the petty-bourgeois city masses toward the Soviet (in 1905) was manifestly sympathetic, even if not very conscious. All the oppressed and aggrieved sought its protection. The popularity of the Soviet spread far beyond the confines of the city. It received "petitions" from peasants who suffered injustices, peasants' resolutions poured into the Soviet, delegations from village communities came to it. Here, right here, is where were concentrated the thoughts and sympathies of the nation, of the real and not the falsified democratic nations'.

In all these quotations—their number can easily be increased two --, three—, and tenfold—the permanent revolution is described as a revolution which welds together the oppressed masses of town and country around the proletariat organized in soviets; as a national revolution that raises the proletariat to power and thereby opens up the possibility of a democratic revolution growing over into the socialist revolution.

The permanent revolution is no isolated leap of the proletariat; rather it is the rebuilding of the whole nation under the leadership of the proletariat. That is how I conceived and interpreted the prospect of the permanent revolution, beginning with 1905.

Radek is also wrong with regard to Parvus[2] -- whose views on the Russian Revolution in 1905 bordered closely on mine, without however being identical with them—when he repeats the stereotyped phrase about Parvus's 'leap' from a Tsarist Government to a Social Democratic one. Radek actually refutes himself when, in another part of his article, he indicates, in passing but quite correctly, wherein my views on the revolution actually differed from those of Parvus. Parvus was not of the opinion that a workers' Government in Russia could move in the direction of the socialist revolution, that is, that in the process of fulfilling the democratic tasks it could grow over into the socialist dictatorship. As is proved by the 1905 quotation adduced by Radek himself, Parvus confined the tasks of the workers' government to the *democratic* tasks. Then where, in that case, is the leap to *socialism*? What Parvus had in mind even at that time was the establishment of a workers' regime after the 'Australian' model, as a consequence of the revolution. Parvus also juxtaposed Russia and Australia after the October Revolution, by which time he himself had already long since taken his stand at the extreme right of social reformism. Bukharin asserted in this connection that Parvus had 'thought up' Australia after the fact, in order to cover up his old aims with regard to the permanent revolution. But that is not so. In 1905, too, Parvus saw in the conquest of power by the proletariat the road to democracy and not to socialism, that is, he assigned to the proletariat only that role which it actually played in Russia in the first eight to ten months of the October Revolution. In further perspective, Parvus even then pointed to the Australian democracy of that time, that is, to a regime in which the workers' party does indeed govern but does not rule, and carries out its reformist demands only as a supplement to the program of the bourgeoisie. By an irony of fate the fundamental tendency of the Right-Centrist bloc of 1923-28 consisted precisely in drawing the dictatorship of the proletariat closer to a workers' democracy of the Australian model, that is, in drawing closer to the prognosis of Parvus. This becomes all the clearer when it is recalled that the Russian petty-bourgeois 'socialists' of two or three decades ago continually depicted Australia in the Russian press as a workers' and peasants' country which, shut off from the outer world by high tariffs, was developing 'socialist' legislation and in that way was building socialism in one country. Radek would have acted correctly had he pushed *this* side of the question to the foreground instead of repeating fairy tales about my fantastic leap over democracy.

Notes

1. I recollect that when Bukharin at the Eighth Plenum of the Executive Committee of the Communist International cited the same quotations, I called to him: 'But there are also directly contrary quotations in Lenin.' After a brief moment of perplexity, Bukharin retorted: 'I know that, I know that, but I am taking what I need, not what you need.' There is the presence of mind of this theoretician for you!—L.T.

2. It should be remembered that at that time Parvus stood at the extreme left of international Marxism.—L.T.

CHAPTER THREE

THREE ELEMENTS OF THE DEMOCRATIC DICTATORSHIP: CLASSES, TASKS AND POLITICAL MECHANICS

The difference between the 'permanent' and the Leninist standpoints expressed itself politically in the counter-posing of the slogan of the dictatorship of the *proletariat* relying on the peasantry to the slogan of the *democratic* dictatorship of the proletariat and the peasantry. The dispute was not concerned with whether the bourgeois-democratic stage could be skipped and whether an alliance between the workers and the peasants was necessary—it concerned the *political mechanics* of the collaboration of the proletariat and the peasantry in the democratic revolution.

Far too presumptuous, not to say light-minded, is Radek's contention that only people 'who have not thought through to the end the complex method of Marxism and Leninism' could raise the question of the *party-political expression* of the democratic dictatorship, whereas Lenin allegedly reduced the whole question to the collaboration of the two classes in the objective historical tasks. No, that is not so.

If in the given question we abstract ourselves from the subjective factor of the revolution: parties and their program—the political and organizational form of the collaboration of proletariat and peasantry—then there will also vanish all the differences of opinion, not only between Lenin and me, which marked two shades of the same revolutionary wing, but what is much worse, also the differences of opinion between Bolshevism and Menshevism, and finally, the differences between the Russian Revolution of 1905 and the Revolutions of 1848 and even of 1789, insofar as the proletariat can at all be spoken of in relation to the latter. *All* bourgeois revolutions were based on the collaboration of the oppressed masses of town and country. That is just what invested the revolutions to a lesser or greater degree with a national character, that is, one embracing the whole people.

The theoretical as well as the political dispute among us was not over the collaboration of the workers and peasants as such, but over the program of this collaboration, its party forms and political methods. In the old revolutions, workers and peasants 'collaborated' under the leadership of the liberal bourgeoisie or its petty-bourgeois democratic wing. The Communist International repeated the experience of the *old* revolutions in a new historical situation by doing everything it could to subject the Chinese workers and peasants to the political leadership of the national liberal Chiang Kai-shek and later of the 'democrat' Wang Ching-wei. Lenin raised the question of an alliance of the workers and peasants irreconcilably opposed to the liberal bourgeoisie. Such an alliance had never before existed in history. It was a matter, so far as its method went, of a new experiment in the collaboration of the oppressed classes of town and country. Thereby the question of the political forms of collaboration was posed anew. Radek has simply overlooked this. That is why he leads us not only back from the formula of the permanent revolution, but also back from Lenin's 'democratic dictatorship'—into an empty historical abstraction.

Yes, Lenin refused for a number of years *to prejudge* the question of what the party-political and state organization of the democratic dictatorship of the proletariat and the peasantry would look like, and he pushed into the foreground the collaboration of these two classes as against a coalition with the liberal bourgeoisie. Lenin said: At a certain historical stage, there inevitably results from the whole objective situation the revolutionary alliance of the working class with the peasantry for the solution of the tasks of the democratic revolution. Will the peasantry be able to create an independent party and will it succeed in doing this? Will this party be in the majority or the minority in the government of the dictatorship? What will be the specific weight of the proletarian representatives in the revolutionary government? None of these questions permits of an *a priori* answer. 'Experience will show!' Insofar as the formula of the democratic dictatorship left half-open the question of the political mechanics of the alliance of workers and peasants, it thereby remained up to a certain point—without in any way becoming transformed into Radek's barren abstraction—an algebraic formula, allowing of extremely divergent political interpretations in the future.

In addition, Lenin himself was in no way of the opinion that the question would be exhausted by the class basis of the dictatorship and its objective historical aims. The significance of the subjective factor—

the aims, the conscious method, the party—Lenin well understood and taught this to all of us. And that is why Lenin in his commentaries on his slogan did not renounce at all an approximate, hypothetical prejudgment of the question of what political forms might be assumed by the first independent alliance of workers and peasants in history. However, Lenin's approach to this question at different times was far from being one and the same. Lenin's thought must not be taken dogmatically but historically. Lenin brought no finished commandments from Mt Sinai, but hammered out ideas and slogans to fit reality, making them concrete and precise, and at different times filled them with different content. But *this side* of the question, which later gained a decisive character and brought the Bolshevik Party to the verge of a split at the beginning of 1917, has not been studied by Radek at all. He has simply ignored it.

It is, however, a fact that Lenin did not always characterize the possible party-political expression and governmental form of the alliance of the two classes in the same way, refraining, however, from binding the party by these hypothetical interpretations. What are the reasons for this caution? The reasons are to be sought in the fact that this algebraic formula contains a quantity, gigantic in significance, but politically extremely indeterminate: *the peasantry.* I want to quote only a few examples of Lenin s interpretation of the democratic dictatorship, with the reservation that a rounded presentation of the *evolution* of Lenin's thought on this question would require a separate work.

Developing the idea that the proletariat and the peasantry would be the basis of the dictatorship, Lenin wrote in March, 1905:

'And such a composition of the social basis of the probable and desirable revolutionary-democratic dictatorship will, of course, find its reflection in the composition of the revolutionary government. *With such a composition the participation or even the predominance of the most diversified representatives of revolutionary democracy in such a government will be inevitable.*'

In these words, Lenin indicates not only the class basis of, but also sketches out a specific governmental form of the dictatorship with a possible predominance of the representatives of petty-bourgeois democracy.

In 1907, Lenin wrote:

'In order to be victorious, the "peasant agrarian revolution" of which you gentlemen speak must, as such, as a peasant revolution, take over the central power throughout the whole state.'

This formula goes even further. It can be understood in the sense that the revolutionary power must be directly concentrated in the hands of the peasantry. But this formula also embraces, in the more far-reaching interpretation introduced into it by the very course of development, the October Revolution which brought the proletariat to power as the 'agent' of the peasant revolution. Such is the amplitude of the possible interpretations of the formula of the democratic dictatorship of the proletariat and the peasantry. We may grant that, up to a certain point, its strong side lay in this algebraic character, but its dangers also lay there, manifesting themselves among us graphically enough after February, and in China leading to catastrophe.

In July 1905, Lenin wrote:

'Nobody speaks of the seizure of power by the party—we speak only of participation, *as far as possible* a leading participation in the revolution....'

In December, 1906, Lenin considered it possible to agree with Kautsky on the question of seizure of power by the party:

'Kautsky considers it not only "as very probable" that "victory will fall to the Social Democratic Party in the course of the revolution," but declares it the duty of the Social Democrats "to instill in their adherents the certainty of victory, for one cannot fight successfully if victory is renounced beforehand".'

The distance between these two interpretations given by Lenin himself is no smaller than between Lenin's formulations and mine. We shall see this even more plainly later on. Here we want to raise the question: What is the meaning of these contradictions in Lenin? They reflect the one and the same 'great unknown' in the political formula of the revolution: *the peasantry*. Not for nothing did the radical thinkers occasionally refer to the peasant as the Sphinx of Russian history. The question of the nature of the revolutionary dictatorship—whether

Radek wishes it or not -- is inseparably bound up with the question of the possibility of a revolutionary peasant party hostile to the liberal bourgeoisie and independent of the proletariat. The decisive meaning of the latter question is not hard to grasp. Were the peasantry capable of creating their own independent party in the epoch of the democratic revolution, then the democratic dictatorship could be realized in its truest and most direct sense, and the question of the participation of the proletarian minority in the revolutionary government would have an important, it is true, but subordinate significance. The case is entirely otherwise if we proceed from the fact that the peasantry, because of its intermediate position and the heterogeneity of its social composition, can have neither an independent policy nor an independent party, but is compelled, in the revolutionary epoch, to choose between the policy of the bourgeoisie and the policy of the proletariat. Only this evaluation of the political nature of the peasantry opens up the prospect of the dictatorship of the proletariat growing directly out of the democratic revolution. In this, naturally, there lies no 'denial', 'ignoring' or 'underestimation' of the peasantry. Without the decisive significance of the agrarian question for the life of the whole of society and without the great depth and gigantic sweep of the peasant revolution there could not even be any talk of the proletarian dictatorship in Russia. But the fact that the *agrarian* revolution created the conditions for the dictatorship *of the proletariat* grew out of the inability of the peasantry to solve its own historical problem with its own forces and under its own leadership. Under present conditions in bourgeois countries, even in the backward ones, insofar as they have already entered the epoch of capitalist industry and are bound into a unit by railroads and telegraphs—this applies not only to Russia but to China and India as well—the peasantry is even less capable of a leading or even only an independent political role than in the epoch of the old bourgeois revolutions. The fact that I invariably and persistently stressed this idea, which forms one of the most important features of the theory of the permanent revolution, also provided a quite inadequate and, in essence, absolutely unfounded pretext for accusing me of underestimating the peasantry.

What were Lenin's views on the question of a peasant party? To reply to this question, a comprehensive review would be required of the evolution of Lenin's views on the Russian revolution in the period of 1905-17. I shall confine myself here to two quotations:

In 1907, Lenin wrote:

'It is possible ... that the objective difficulties of a political unification of the petty bourgeoisie will check the formation of such a party and leave the peasant democracy for a long time in the present state of a spongy, shapeless, pulpy, Trudoviki-like[1] mass.'

In 1909, Lenin expressed himself on the same theme in a different way:

'There is not the slightest doubt that a revolution which reaches. . . so high a degree of development as the revolutionary dictatorship will create a more firmly-formed and more powerful revolutionary peasant party. To judge the matter otherwise would mean to assume that in a grown-up man, the size, form and degree of development of certain essential organs could remain in a childish state.'

Was this assumption confirmed? No, it was not. But that is just what Induced Lenin, *up to the moment of the complete verification by history*, to give an algebraic answer to the question of the revolutionary government. Naturally, Lenin never put his hypothetical formula above the reality. The struggle for the independent political party of the proletariat constituted the main content of his life. The woeful epigones, however, in their hunt after a peasant party, ended up with the subordination of the Chinese workers to the Kuomintang, the strangulation of communism in India in the name of the 'Workers' and Peasants' Party', the dangerous fiction of the Peasants' International, the masquerade of the League Against Imperialism, and so on.

Prevailing official thought makes no effort to dwell on the contradictions in Lenin adduced above, which are in part external and apparent, in part real, but which always stem from the problem itself. Now that there have arisen among us a special species of 'Red' professors who are frequently distinguished from the old reactionary professors not by a firmer backbone but only by a profounder ignorance, Lenin is professorially trimmed and purged of all contradictions, that is, of the dynamics of his thought; standard quotations are threaded on separate threads, and then one 'series' or another set in circulation, according to the requirements of the 'current moment'.

It must not be forgotten for a moment that the problems of the revolution in a politically 'virgin' country became acute after a great historical interval, after a lengthy reactionary epoch in Europe and in the whole world, and for that reason alone contained many unknowns. Through the formula of the democratic dictatorship of the workers and peasants, Lenin expressed the peculiarity of Russian social conditions. He gave different interpretations to this formula, but did not reject it until he had probed to the end the peculiar conditions of the Russian revolution. Wherein lay this peculiarity?

The gigantic role of the agrarian question and the peasant question in general, as the soil or the subsoil of all other problems, and the great number of the peasant intellectuals and those who sympathized with the peasants, with their Narodnik ideology, with their 'anti-capitalist' traditions and their revolutionary tempering—all this in its entirety signified that *if an anti-bourgeois revolutionary peasant party was at all possible anywhere, then it was possible precisely and primarily in Russia* . And as a matter of fact, in the endeavors to create a peasant party, or a workers' and peasants' party—as distinct from a liberal or a proletarian party— every possible political variant was attempted in Russia, illegal and parliamentary as well as a combination of the two: *Zemlya i Volya* (Land and Freedom), *Narodnaya Volya* (People's Will), *Cherny Peredel* (Black Redistribution), the legal *Narodnichestvo* (Populists), 'Socialist-Revolutionaries', 'People's Socialists', 'Trudoviks', 'Left Socialist-Revolutionaries', etc., etc. For half a century we had, as it were, a huge laboratory for the creation of an 'anti-capitalist' peasant party with an independent position toward the proletarian party. The largest scope was attained, as is well known, by the experiment of the S.R. Party which, for a time in 1917, actually constituted the party of the overwhelming majority of the peasantry. But what happened? This party used its position only to betray the peasants completely to the liberal bourgeoisie. The Socialist-Revolutionaries entered into a coalition with the imperialists of the Entente and together with them conducted an armed struggle against the Russian proletariat.

This truly classic experiment shows that petty-bourgeois parties based on the peasantry are still able to retain a semblance of independent policy during the humdrum periods of history when secondary questions are on the agenda; but when the revolutionary crisis of society puts the fundamental questions of property on the order of the day, the petty-bourgeois 'peasant' party automatically becomes a tool in the hands of the bourgeoisie against the proletariat.

If my old differences of opinion with Lenin are analyzed not on the plane of quotations indiscriminately torn out of this and that year, month and day, but in their correct historical perspective, then it becomes quite clear that the dispute, at least on my part, was not over whether an alliance of the proletariat with the peasants was required for the solution of the democratic tasks, but over what party-political and state form the revolutionary cooperation of the proletariat and the peasantry could assume, and what consequences could result from it for the further development of the revolution. I speak of course of my position in this dispute, not of the position of Bukharin and Radek at that time, for which they themselves must answer.

How close the formula of the 'permanent revolution' approximated to Lenin's formula is graphically illustrated by the following comparison. In the summer of 1905, that is, before the October general strike and before the December uprising in Moscow, I wrote in the foreword to one of Lassalle's speeches:

'It is self-evident that the proletariat, as in its time the bourgeoisie, fulfills its mission supported by the peasantry and the urban petty bourgeoisie. The proletariat leads the countryside, draws it into the movement, gives it an interest in the success of its plans. The proletariat, however, unavoidably remains the leader. This is not "the dictatorship of the peasantry and proletariat" but *the dictatorship of the proletariat supported by the peasantry*'.[2]

Now compare these words, written in 1905 and quoted by me in the Polish article of 1909, with the following words of Lenin written likewise in 1909, just after the party conference, under the pressure of Rosa Luxemburg, had adopted the formula 'dictatorship of the proletariat supported by the peasantry' instead of the old Bolshevik formula. To the Mensheviks, who spoke of the radical change of Lenin's position, the latter replied:

... The formula which the Bolsheviks have here chosen for themselves reads: *"the proletariat which leads the peasantry behind it."*[3]

'... Isn't it obvious that the idea of all these formulations is one and the same? Isn't it obvious that this idea expresses precisely the dictatorship of the proletariat and peasantry—that the *"formula" of the proletariat supported by the peasantry, remains entirely within the bounds of that very same dictatorship of the proletariat and peasantry?*'

Thus Lenin puts a construction on the 'algebraic' formula here which excludes the idea of an *independent* peasant party and even more its dominant role in the revolutionary government: the proletariat leads the peasantry, the proletariat is *supported* by the peasantry, consequently the revolutionary power is concentrated in the hands of the party of the proletariat. But this is precisely the central point of the theory of the permanent revolution.

Today, that is, *after* the historical test has taken place, the utmost that can be said about the old differences of opinion on the question of the dictatorship is the following:

While Lenin, always proceeding from the leading role of the proletariat, emphasized and developed in every way the necessity of the revolutionary democratic collaboration of the workers and peasants—teaching this to all of us—I, invariably proceeding from this collaboration, emphasized in every way the necessity of proletarian leadership, not only in the bloc but also in the government which would be called upon to head this bloc. No other differences can be read into the matter.

In connexion with the foregoing, let us take two quotations: one out of 'Results and Prospects', which Stalin and Zinoviev utilized to prove the antagonism between my views and Lenin's, the other out of a polemical article by Lenin against me, which Radek employs for the same purpose.

Here is the first quotation:

'The participation of the proletariat in a government is also objectively most probable, and permissible on principle, only as a *dominating and leading participation*. One may, of course, describe such a government as the dictatorship of the proletariat and peasantry, a dictatorship of the proletariat, peasantry and intelligentsia, or even a coalition government of the working class and the petty bourgeoisie, but the question nevertheless remains: who is to wield the hegemony in the government itself, and through it, in the country? And when we speak of a workers' government, by this we reply that the hegemony should belong to the working class.'

Zinoviev (in 1925!) raised a hue and cry because I (in 1905!) had placed the peasantry and the intelligentsia on the same plane. He got nothing else from the above-cited lines. The reference to the intelligentsia resulted from the conditions of that period, during which the intelligentsia played politically an entirely different role from that which it plays today. Only exclusively intellectual organizations spoke at that time in the name of the peasantry; the Socialist-Revolutionaries officially built their party on the 'triad': proletariat, peasantry, intelligentsia; the Mensheviks, as I wrote at that time, clutched at the heels of every radical intellectual in order to prove the blossoming of bourgeois democracy. I expressed myself hundreds of times in those days on the impotence of the intellectuals as an 'independent' social group and on the decisive significance of the revolutionary peasantry.

But after all, we are certainly not discussing here a single polemical phrase, which I have no intention at all of defending. The essence of the quotation is this: that I completely accept the Leninist content of the democratic dictatorship and only demand a more precise definition of its political mechanism, that is, the exclusion of the sort of coalition in which the proletariat would only be a hostage amid a petty-bourgeois majority.

Now let us examine Lenin's 1916 article which, as Radek himself points out, was directed *formally* against Trotsky, but *in reality* against Bukharin, Pyatakov, the writer of these lines (that is, Radek) and a number of other comrades'. This is a very valuable admission, which entirely confirms my impression of that time that Lenin was directing the polemic against me only in appearance, for the content, as I shall demonstrate forthwith, did not in reality at all refer to me. This article contains (in two lines) that very accusation concerning my alleged 'denial of the peasantry' which later became the main capital of the epigones and their disciples. The 'nub' of this article—as Radek puts it—is the following passage:

'Trotsky has not taken into consideration,' says Lenin, quoting my own words, 'that if the proletariat draws behind it the non-proletarian masses of the village to confiscate the landlords' estates and overthrow the monarchy, then this will constitute the consummation of the "national bourgeois revolution", and that in Russia this is just what the *revolutionary democratic dictatorship of the proletariat and the peasantry will be*.

That Lenin did not direct to the 'right address' this reproach of my 'denial' of the peasantry, but really meant Bukharin and Radek, who actually did skip over the democratic stage of the revolution is clear not only from everything that has been said above, but also from the quotation adduced by Radek himself, which he rightly calls the 'nub' of Lenin's article. In point of fact, *Lenin directly quotes the words of my article to the effect that only an independent and bold policy of the proletariat can 'draw behind it the non-proletarian masses of the village to confiscates the landlords' estates and overthrow the monarchy'*, etc. and then Lenin adds: 'Trotsky has not taken into consideration that ... this is just what the revolutionary democratic dictatorship will be.' In other words, Lenin confirms here and, so to speak, certifies that Trotsky in reality accepts the whole actual content of the Bolshevik formula (the collaboration of the workers and peasants and the democratic tasks of this collaboration), but refuses to recognize that this is just what the democratic dictatorship, the consummation of the national revolution, will be. It therefore follows that the dispute in this apparently 'sharp' polemical article involves not the program of the next stage of the revolution and its driving class forces, but precisely the *political correlation of these forces, the political and party character of the dictatorship*. While, as a result in part of the unclarity at that time of the processes themselves and in part of factional exaggerations, polemical misunderstandings were comprehensible and unavoidable in those days, it is completely incomprehensible how Radek contrived to introduce such confusion into the question after the event.

My polemic with Lenin was waged in essence over the possibility of the independence (and the degree of the independence) of the peasantry in the revolution, particularly over the possibility of an independent peasants' party. In this polemic, I accused Lenin of overestimating the *independent* role of the peasantry. Lenin accused me of underestimating the *revolutionary* role of the peasantry. This flowed from the logic of the polemic itself. But is it not contemptible for anyone today, two decades later, to use these old quotations, tearing them out of the context of the party relationships of that time and investing each polemical exaggeration or episodic error with an absolute meaning, instead of laying bare in the light of the very great revolutionary experience we have had what the actual axis of the differences was and what was the real and not verbal scope of these differences?

Compelled to limit myself in the selection of quotations, I shall refer here only to the summary theses of Lenin on the stages of the revolution, which were written at the end of 1905 but only published for the first time in 1926 in the fifth volume of *Lenin Miscellanies*. I recall that all the Oppositionists, Radek included, regarded the publication of these theses as the handsomest of gifts to the Opposition, for Lenin turned out in these theses to be guilty of 'Trotskyism' in accordance with all the articles of the Stalinist code. The most important points of the resolution of the Seventh Plenum of the E.C.C.I. which condemns Trotskyism seem to be avowedly and deliberately directed against the fundamental theses of Lenin. The Stalinists gnashed their teeth in rage at their publication. The Editor of this volume of the *Miscellanies*, Kamenev, told me flatly with the not very bashful 'good nature' that is characteristic of him that if a bloc between us were not being prepared he would never under any circumstances have allowed the publication of this document. Finally, in an article by Kostrzewa in *Bolshevik*, these theses were fraudulently falsified precisely to spare Lenin from being charged with Trotskyism in his attitude toward the peasantry as a whole and the middle peasant in particular.

In addition I quote here Lenin's own evaluation of his differences of opinion with me, which he made in 1909:

'Comrade Trotsky himself, in this instance, grants "the participation of the representatives of the democratic population" in the "workers' government," that is, *he grants a government of representatives of the proletariat and the peasantry*. Under what conditions the participation of the proletariat in the revolutionary government is permissible is a separate question, and on this question, the Bolsheviks will most likely fail to see eye to eye not only with Trotsky but also with the Polish Social Democrats. The question of the dictatorship of the revolutionary classes, however, is in no case reducible to the question of the "majority" in this or that revolutionary government, or to the conditions under which the participation of the Social Democrats in this or that government is permissible.

In this quotation from Lenin, it is again confirmed that Trotsky accepts a government of representatives of the proletariat and the peasantry, and therefore does not 'skip over' the latter. Lenin furthermore emphasizes that the question of the dictatorship is not reducible to the question of the majority of the government. This is altogether beyond dispute. What is involved here, first and foremost, is the joint struggle of the proletariat and peasantry and consequently the struggle of the proletarian vanguard against the liberal or national bourgeoisie for influence over the peasants. But while the question of the revolutionary dictatorship of the workers and peasants is *not reducible* to the question of this or that majority in the government, nevertheless, upon the victory of the revolution, this question inescapably *arises* as the decisive one. As we have seen, Lenin makes a cautious reservation (against all eventualities) to the effect that should matters reach the point of participation by the party in the revolutionary government, then perhaps differences might arise with Trotsky and the Polish comrades *over the conditions* of this participation. It was a matter therefore of *possible* difference of opinion, insofar as Lenin considered theoretically permissible the participation of the representatives of the proletariat as a minority in a democratic government. Events, however, showed that no differences arose between us. In November, 1917, a bitter struggle flared up in the top leadership of the party over the question of the coalition government with the Socialist-Revolutionaries and the Mensheviks. Lenin, without objecting in principle to a coalition on the basis of the soviets, categorically demanded that the Bolshevik majority be firmly safeguarded. I stood shoulder to shoulder with Lenin.

Now let us hear from Radek. To just what does he reduce the whole question of the democratic dictatorship of the proletariat and the peasantry?

'Wherein,' he asks, 'did the old **Bolshevik** theory of 1905 prove to be fundamentally correct? In the fact that the joint action of the Petrograd workers and peasants (the soldiers of the Petrograd garrison) overthrew Tsarism (in 1917—L.T.). After all, the 1905 formula foresees in its fundamentals only the correlation of classes, and not a concrete political institution.'

Just a minute, please! By designating the old Leninist formula as 'algebraic,' I do not imply that it is permissible to reduce it to an empty commonplace, as Radek does so thoughtlessly. 'The fundamental thing was realized: the proletariat and the peasantry jointly overthrew Tsarism.' But this 'fundamental thing' was realized without exception in all victorious or semi-victorious revolutions. Tsars, feudal lords, and priests were always and everywhere beaten with the fists of the proletarians or the precursors of the proletarians, the plebeians and peasants. This happened as early as the 16th century in Germany and even earlier. In China it was also workers and peasants who beat down the 'militarists.' What has this to do with the democratic dictatorship? Such a dictatorship never arose in the old revolutions, nor did it arise in the Chinese revolution. Why not? Because astride the backs of the workers and peasants, who did the rough work of the revolution, sat the bourgeoisie. Radek has abstracted himself so violently from 'political institutions' that he has forgotten the 'most fundamental thing' in a revolution, namely, who leads it and who seizes power. A revolution, however, is a struggle for power. It is a political struggle which the classes wage *not* with bare hands but through the medium of 'political institutions' (parties, etc.).

'People who have not thought out to the end the complexity of the method of Marxism and Leninism', Radek thunders against us sinners, entertain the following conception: 'The whole thing must invariably end in a joint government of workers and peasants; and some even think that this must invariably be a coalition government of workers' and peasants' parties.'

What blockheads these 'some' are! And what does Radek himself think? Does he think that a victorious revolution is not bound to reflect and set its seal upon a specific correlation of revolutionary classes? Radek has deepened the 'sociological' problem to the point where nothing remains of it but a verbalistic shell.

How impermissible it is to abstract oneself from the question of the political forms of the collaboration of the workers and peasants will best be shown to us by the following words from an address by the same Radek to the Communist Academy in March, 1927 :

'A year ago, I wrote an article in *Pravda* on this (Canton) government designating it as a *peasants' and workers' government*. A comrade of the editorial board assumed that it was an oversight on my part and changed it to *workers' and peasants' government*. I did not protest against this and let it stand: workers' and peasants' government.'

Thus, in March, 1927 (not in 1905), Radek was of the opinion that there could be a peasants' and workers' government in contradistinction to a workers' and peasants' government. This was beyond the editor of *Pravda*. I confess that for the life of me I can't understand it either. We know well what a workers' and peasants' government is. But what is a peasants' and workers' government, in contrast and as opposed to a workers' and peasants' government? Please be so kind as to explain this mysterious transposition of adjectives. Here we touch the very heart of the question. In 1926, Radek believed the Canton government of Chiang Kai-shek was a peasants' and workers' government. In 1927 he repeated this formula. In reality, however, it proved to be a *bourgeois* government, exploiting the revolutionary struggle of the workers and peasants and then drowning them in blood. How is this error to be explained? Did Radek simply misjudge? From far away it is easy to misjudge. Then why not say it: I did not understand, could not see, I made a mistake. But no, this is no factual error due to lack of information, but rather, as is now clear, a profound mistake in principle. The peasants' and workers' government, as opposed to the workers' and peasants' government, is nothing else but the Kuomintang. It can mean nothing else. If the peasantry does not follow the proletariat, it follows the bourgeoisie. I believe that this question has been sufficiently clarified in my criticism of the factional Stalinist idea of a 'two-class, worker-peasant party' (see *The Draft Programme of the Communist International; A Criticism of Fundamentals*).The Canton 'peasants' and workers' government', in contrast to a workers' and peasants' government, is also the only conceivable expression, in the language of present-day Chinese politics, of the 'democratic dictatorship' as opposed to the proletarian dictatorship; in other words, the embodiment of the

Stalinist Kuomintang policy as opposed to the Bolshevik policy which the Communist International labels 'Trotskyist'.

Notes

1. The Trudoviks were representatives of the peasants in the four Dumas, constantly vacillating between the Cadets (Liberals) and the Social Democrats.—L.T.

2. This quotation, among a hundred others, shows in passing that I did have an inkling of the existence of the peasantry and the importance of the agrarian question as far back as the eve of the 1905 Revolution, that is, some time before the significance of the peasantry was explained to me by Maslov, Thalheimer, Thaelmann, Remmele, Cachin, Monmousseau, Bela Kun, Pepper, Kuusinen and the other Marxist sociologists.—L.T.

3. At the 1909 Conference, Lenin proposed the formula of 'the proletariat which leads the peasantry behind it,' but in the end he associated himself with the formula of the Polish Social Democrats, which won the majority at the conference against the Mensheviks.—L.T.

CHAPTER FOUR

WHAT DID THE THEORY OF THE PERMANENT REVOLUTION LOOK LIKE IN PRACTICE?

In his criticism of our theory, Radek adds to it, as we have seen, also the *'tactic derived from it'*. This is a very important addition. The official Stalinist criticism of 'Trotskyism' on this question prudently limited itself to theory ... For Radek, however, this does not suffice. He is conducting a struggle against a definite (Bolshevik) tactical line in China. He seeks to discredit this line by the theory of the permanent revolution, and to do this he must show, or pretend that somebody else has already shown, that a false tactical line has in the past flowed from this theory. Here Radek is directly misleading his readers. It is possible that he himself in unfamiliar with the history of the revolution, in which he never took a direct part. But apparently he has not made the slightest effort to examine the question through documents. Yet the most important of these are contained in the second volume of my *Collected Works*. They can be checked by anyone who can read. And so, let me inform Radek that virtually throughout all the stages of the first revolution I was in complete solidarity with Lenin in evaluating the forces of the revolution and its successive tasks, in spite of the fact that I spent the whole of 1905 living illegally in Russia, and 1906 in prison. I am compelled to confine myself here to a minimum of proofs and documentation.

In an article written in February and printed in March, 1905, that is, two or three months before the first Bolshevik Congress (which is recorded in history as the Third Party Congress), I wrote :

'The bitter struggle between the people and the Tsar, which knows no other thought than victory; the all-national insurrection as the culminating point of this struggle; the provisional government as the revolutionary culmination of the victory of the people over their age-old foe; the disarming of the Tsarist reaction and the arming of the people by the provisional government; the convocation of the constituent assembly on the basis of universal, I equal, direct and secret suffrage—these are the objectively indicated stages of the revolution.' (*Collected Works*, Volume II, Part I.)

It is enough to compare these words with the resolutions of the Bolshevik Congress of May, 1905, in order to recognize in the formulation my complete solidarity with the Bolsheviks on the fundamental problems.

Nor is this all. In harmony with this article, I formulated in Petersburg, in agreement with Krassin, the theses on the provisional government which appeared illegally at that time. Krassin defended them at the Bolshevik Congress. The following words of Lenin show how much he approved of them:

'I share entirely the views of Comrade Krassin. It is natural that, as a writer, I gave attention to the literary formulation of the question. *The importance of the aim* of the struggle has been shown very correctly by Comrade Krassin, and *I am with him completely*. One cannot engage in struggle without reckoning on capturing the position for which one is fighting. ... '

The major part of Krassin's extensive amendment, to which I refer the reader, was embodied in the Congress resolution. That I was the author of this amendment is proved by a note from Krassin, which I still possess. This whole episode in the history of the Party is well known to Kamenev and others.

The problem of the peasantry, the problem of drawing the peasantry close to the workers' soviets, of coordinating work with the Peasants' League, engaged the attention of the Petersburg Soviet more and more every day. Is Radek perhaps aware that the leadership of the Soviet devolved upon me? Here is one of the hundreds of formulations I wrote at that time on the tactical tasks of the revolution:

'The proletariat creates city-wide "soviets" which direct the fighting actions of the urban masses, and puts upon the order of the day the fighting alliance with the army and the peasantry.' (*Nachalo*, No. 4. November 17 [new style, November 30], 1905.)

It is boring, and even embarrassing, let me confess, to cite quotations proving that I never even talked of a 'leap' from autocracy into Socialism. But it can't be helped. I wrote the following, for example, in February, 1906, on the tasks of the Constituent Assembly, without in any way counter-posing the latter to the **soviets**, as Radek, following Stalin, now hastens to do in regard to China in order to sweep away with an ultra-leftist broom all traces of yesterday's opportunist policy:

'The liberated people will convoke the Constituent Assembly by its own power. The tasks of the Constituent Assembly will be gigantic. It will have to reconstruct the State upon democratic principles, that is, upon the principles of the absolute sovereignty of the people. Its duty will be to organize a people's militia, carry through a vast agrarian (land) reform, and introduce the eight-hour day and a graduated income tax. (*Collected Works*, Volume II, Part I.)

And here is what I wrote, in 1905, in an agitational leaflet, specifically on the question of the 'immediate' introduction of socialism :

'Is it thinkable to introduce socialism in Russia immediately? No, our countryside is far too benighted and unconscious. There are still too few real socialists among the peasants. We must first overthrow the autocracy, which keeps the masses of the people in darkness. The rural poor must be freed of all taxation; the graduated progressive income tax, universal compulsory education, must be introduced; finally, the rural proletariat and semi-proletariat must be fused with the town proletariat into a single social democratic army. Only this army can accomplish the great socialist revolution.' (*Collected Works*, Volume II, Part 1.)

It therefore follows that I did differentiate somewhat between the democratic and socialist stages of the revolution, long before Radek, tailing after Stalin and Thaelmann, began lecturing me on this subject. Twenty-two years ago, I wrote;

'When the idea of uninterrupted revolution was formulated in the socialist press—an idea which connected the liquidation of absolutism and feudalism with a socialist revolution, along with growing social conflicts, uprisings of new sections of the masses, unceasing attacks by the proletariat upon economic and political privileges of the ruling classes—our "progressive" press raised a unanimous howl of indignation.' (*Our Revolution*, 1906.)

First of all, I should like to call attention to the definition of the uninterrupted revolution contained in these words: it connects the liquidation of medievalism with the socialist revolution through a number of sharpening social clashes. Where then is the leap? Where is the ignoring of the democratic stage? And after all, isn't this what actually happened in 1917?

It is noteworthy, by the way, that the howl raised by the 'progressive' press in 1905 over the uninterrupted revolution can in no wise be compared with the hardly progressive howling of the present-day hacks who have intervened in the affair after a brief delay of a quarter of a century.

What was the attitude of the then leading organ of the Bolshevik faction, *Novaya Zhizn*, published under the vigilant editorship of Lenin, when I raised the question of the permanent revolution in the press? Surely, this point is not devoid of interest. To an article of the 'radical' bourgeois newspaper *Nasha Zhizn (Our Life)*, which endeavored to set up the 'more rational' views of Lenin against the 'permanent revolution' of Trotsky, the **Bolshevik** *Novaya Zhizn* replied (on November 27, 1905) as follows:

'This gratuitous assumption is of course sheer nonsense. Comrade Trotsky said that the proletarian revolution can, without halting at the first stage, continue on its road, elbowing the exploiters aside; Lenin, on the other hand, pointed out that the political revolution is only the first step. The publicist of *Nasha Zhizn* would like to see a contradiction here.... The whole misunderstanding comes, first, from the fear with which the name alone of the social revolution fills *Nasha Zhizn*; secondly, out of the desire of this paper to discover some sort of sharp and piquant difference of opinion among the Social Democrats; and thirdly, in the figure of speech used by Comrade Trotsky: "at a single blow." In No. 10 of *Nachalo*, Comrade Trotsky explains his idea quite unambiguously:

"The complete victory of the revolution signifies the victory of the proletariat", writes Comrade Trotsky. "But this victory in turn implies the uninterruptedness of the revolution in the future. The proletariat realizes in life the fundamental democratic tasks, and the very logic of its immediate struggle to consolidate its political rule poses before the proletariat, at a certain moment, purely socialist problems. Between the minimum and the maximum program (of the Social Democrats) a revolutionary continuity is established. It is not a question of a single 'blow', or of a single day or month, but of a whole historical epoch. It would be absurd to try to fix its duration in advance."'

This one reference in a way exhausts the subject of the present pamphlet. What refutation of the entire subsequent criticism by the epigones could be more clear, precise and incontrovertible than this refutation contained in my newspaper article so approvingly quoted by Lenin's *Novaya Zhizn*? My article explained that the victorious proletariat, in the process of carrying out the democratic tasks, would by the logic of its position inevitably be confronted at a certain stage by purely socialist problems. That is just where the *continuity* lies between the minimum and the maximum programs, which grows inevitably out of the dictatorship of the proletariat. This is not a single blow, it is not a leap—I explained to my critics in the camp of the petty bourgeoisie of that time—it is a whole historical epoch. And Lenin's *Novaya Zhizn* associated itself completely with this prospect. Even more important, I hope, is the fact that it was verified by the actual course of development and in 1917 was decisively confirmed as correct.

Apart from the petty-bourgeois democrats of *Nasha Zhizn*, it was mainly the Mensheviks who in 1905, and particularly in 1906 after the defeat of the revolution had begun, spoke of the fantastic 'leap' over democracy to socialism. Among the Mensheviks it was especially Martynov and the late Yordansky who distinguished themselves in this held. Both of them, be it said in passing later became stalwart Stalinists. To the Menshevik writers who sought to hang the 'leap to socialism' on me, I expounded, in a special article written in 1906, in detail and in popular style, not only the error but also the stupidity of such a contention. I could reprint this article today, almost unabridged, against the criticism of the epigones. But it will perhaps suffice to say that the conclusion of this article was summed up in the following words :

'I understand perfectly—let me assure my reviewer (Yordansky) -- that to leap, in a newspaper article, over a political obstacle is far from the same as surmounting it in practice.' (*Collected Works*, Volume II, Part 1.)

Perhaps this will suffice? If not, I can continue, so that critics like Radek will not be able to say that they did not have 'at hand' the material on which they pass judgment so cavalierly.

Our Tactics, a small pamphlet which I wrote in prison in 1906, and which was immediately published by Lenin, contains the following characteristic conclusion:

'The proletariat will be able to support itself upon the uprising of the village, and in the towns, the centers of political life, it will be able to carry through to a victorious conclusion the cause which it has been able to initiate. Supporting itself upon the elemental forces of the peasantry, and leading the latter, the proletariat will not only deal reaction the final triumphant blow, but it will also know how to secure the victory of the revolution.' (*Collected Works*, Volume II, Part 1.)

Does this smack of ignoring the peasantry? In the same pamphlet, by the way, the following idea also is developed:

'Our tactics, calculated upon the irresistible development of the revolution, must not of course ignore the inevitable or the possible or even only the probable phases and stages of the revolutionary movement.' (*Collected Works*, Volume II, Part 1.)

Does this look like a fantastic leap?

In my article, *The Lessons of the First Soviet* (1906), I depict the prospects for the further development of the revolution (or, as it turned out in reality, for the new revolution) in the following manner:

'History does not repeat itself—and the new **Soviet** will not have once more to go through the events of the fifty days (October to December 1905); instead, it will be able to borrow its program of action completely from this period. This program is perfectly clear. Revolutionary co-operation with the army, the peasantry, and the lowest plebeian strata of the urban petty bourgeoisie. Abolition of the autocracy. Destruction of its material organization: in part through reorganization and in part through the immediate dissolution of the army; destruction of the bureaucratic police apparatus. Eight-hour day. Arming of the population, above all of the proletariat. Transformation of the soviets into organs of revolutionary urban self-administration. Creation of soviets of peasants' deputies (peasant committees) as organs of the agrarian revolution in the localities. Organization of elections to the Constituent Assembly, and electoral struggle on the basis of a definite program of action for the people's representatives.' (*Collected Works*, Volume II Part 2.)

Does this look like skipping over the agrarian revolution, or underestimation of the peasant question as a whole? Does this look as though I was blind to the democratic tasks of the revolution? No, it does not. But what then does the political picture drawn by Radek look like? Nothing at all. Magnanimously, but very ambiguously, Radek draws a line between my 1905 position, which he distorts, and the position of the Mensheviks, without suspecting that he is himself repeating three-fourths of the Menshevik criticism; even though Trotsky, to be sure, employed the same methods as the Mensheviks, Radek explains jesuitically, his aim was nevertheless different. By this subjective formula, Radek completely discredits his own approach to the question. Even Lassalle knew that the end depends upon the means and in the final analysis is conditioned by it. He even wrote a play on this subject (*Franz Von Sickingen*). But what is it that renders my means and that of the Mensheviks one and the same? The attitude towards the peasantry. As evidence, Radek adduces three polemical lines from the above-cited 1916 article by Lenin, observing in passing, however, that here Lenin, although he names Trotsky, was in reality polemicizing against Bukharin and against Radek himself. Besides this quotation from Lenin which, as we have already seen, is refuted by the whole content of Lenin's article, Radek makes reference to Trotsky himself. Exposing the emptiness Of the Menshevik conception, I asked in my 1916 article: If it is not the liberal bourgeoisie that will lead, then who will? After all, you Mensheviks do not in any case believe in the *independent* political role of the peasantry. So then, Radek has caught me red-handed: Trotsky 'agreed' with the Mensheviks about the role of the peasantry. The Mensheviks held it impermissible to 'repulse' the liberal bourgeoisie for the sake of a dubious and unreliable alliance with the peasantry. This was the 'method' of the Mensheviks; while mine consisted of brushing aside the liberal bourgeoisie and fighting for the leadership of the revolutionary peasantry. On this fundamental question I had no differences with Lenin. And when I said to the Mensheviks in the course of the struggle against them: 'You are in any case not inclined to assign a *leading* role to the peasantry, then this was not an agreement with the method of the Mensheviks as Radek tries to insinuate, but only the clear posing of an alternative: *either* the dictatorship of the liberal plutocracy *or* the dictatorship of the proletariat.

The same completely correct argument put forward by me in 1916 against the Mensheviks, which Radek now disloyally tries to utilize against me also, had been used by me nine years earlier, at the London Congress of 1907, when I defended the theses of the Bolsheviks on the attitude toward non-proletarian parties. I quote here the essential part of my London speech which, in the first years of the revolution, was often reprinted in anthologies and textbooks as the expression of the Bolshevik attitude toward classes and parties in the revolution. Here is what I said in this speech, which contains a succinct formulation of the theory of the permanent revolution.

'To the Menshevik comrades, their own views appear extremely complex. I have repeatedly heard accusations from them that my conception of the course of the Russian revolution is oversimplified. And yet, despite their extreme amorphousness, which is one of the forms of complexity,—and perhaps just because of this amorphousness—the views of the **Mensheviks** fall into a very simple pattern comprehensible even to Mr. Milyukov. 'In a postscript to the recent published book, *How Did The Elections To The Second State Duma Turn Out?* the ideological leader of the Cadet Party writes: "As to the left groups in the narrower sense of the word, that is, the socialist and revolutionary groups, an agreement with them will be more difficult. But even here again, there are, if no definite positive reasons, then at least some very weighty negative ones which can to a certain extent facilitate an agreement between us. Their aim is to criticize and to discredit us; for that reason alone it is necessary that we be present and act. As we know, to the socialists, not only in Russia but throughout the world, the revolution now taking place is a bourgeois and not a socialist revolution. It is a revolution which is to be accomplished by bourgeois democracy. To supersede this democracy ... is something no socialists in the whole world are ready to do, and if the country has sent them into the Duma in such great numbers, then it was certainly not for the purpose of realizing socialism now or in order to carry through the preparatory 'bourgeois' reforms with their own hands ... It will be far more advantageous for them to leave the role of parliamentarians to us than to compromise themselves in this role."

'As we see, Milyukov brings us straight to the heart of the question. The quotation cited gives all the most important elements of the Menshevik attitude toward the revolution and the relationship between bourgeois and socialist democracy.

'The revolution that is taking place is a bourgeois and not a socialist revolution"—that's the first and most important point. The bourgeois revolution "must be accomplished by the bourgeois democracy"—that's the second point. The socialist democracy cannot carry through bourgeois reforms with its own hands, its role remains purely oppositional: "Criticize and discredit." This is the third point. And finally—as the fourth point—in order to enable the socialists to remain in the opposition, "it is necessary that we (that is, the bourgeois democracy) be present and act."

'But what if "we" are not present? And what if there is no bourgeois democracy capable of marching at the head of the bourgeois revolution? Then it must be invented. This is just the conclusion to which Menshevism arrives. It produces bourgeois democracy, its attributes and history, out of its own imagination.

'As materialists, we must first of all pose the question of the social bases of bourgeois democracy: upon what strata or classes can it rest?

'As a revolutionary force the big bourgeoisie can be dismissed—we all agree on this. Even at the time of the Great French Revolution, which was a national revolution in the broadest sense, certain Lyons industrialists played a counter-revolutionary role. But we are told of the middle bourgeoisie, and also and primarily of the petty bourgeoisie, as being the leading force of the bourgeois revolution. But what does this petty bourgeoisie represent?

'The Jacobins based themselves upon the urban democracy, which had grown out of the craft guilds. Small masters, journeymen, and the town population closely bound up with them, constituted the army of the revolutionary sansculottes, the prop of the leading party of the Montagnards. It was precisely this compact mass of the city population, which had gone through the long historical school of the craft guilds that bore upon its shoulders the whole burden of the revolution. The objective result of the revolution was the creation of 'normal' conditions of capitalist exploitation. The social mechanics of the historical process, however, produced this result, that the conditions for bourgeois domination were created by the 'mob', the democracy of the streets, the sansculottes. Their terrorist dictatorship purged bourgeois society of the old rubbish and then, after it had overthrown the dictatorship of the petty-bourgeois democracy, the bourgeoisie came to power.

'Now I ask—alas, not for the first time!—what social class in our country will raise up revolutionary bourgeois democracy, put it in power, and make it possible-for it to carry out gigantic tasks, if the proletariat remains in opposition? This is the central question, and I again put it to the Mensheviks.

'It is true, in our country there are huge masses of the revolutionary peasantry. But the Menshevik comrades know just as well as I do that the peasantry, regardless of how revolutionary it may be, is incapable of playing an *independent*, much less a *leading* political role. The peasantry can undoubtedly prove to be a tremendous force in the service of the revolution; but it would be unworthy of a Marxist to believe that a peasant party is capable of placing itself at the head of a bourgeois revolution and, upon its own initiative, liberating the nation's productive forces from the archaic fetters that weigh upon them. The town is the hegemon in modern society and only the town is capable of assuming the role of hegemon in the bourgeois revolution.[1]

'Now, where is the urban democracy in our country capable of leading the nation behind it? Comrade Martynov has already sought it repeatedly, magnifying-glass in hand. He discovered Saratov teachers, Petersburg lawyers, and Moscow statisticians. Like all his co-thinkers, the only thing that he refused to notice was that in the Russian revolution the industrial proletariat has conquered the very same ground as was occupied by the semi-proletarian artisan democracy of the sansculottes at the end of the eighteenth century. I call your attention, Comrades, to this fundamental fact.

'Our large-scale industry did not grow organically out of the crafts. The economic history of our towns knows absolutely nothing of any period of guilds. Capitalist industry arose in our country under the direct and immediate pressure of European capital. It took possession of a soil essentially virginal, primitive, without encountering any resistance from craft culture. Foreign capital flowed into our country through the channels of state loans and through the pipe-lines of private initiative. It gathered around itself the army of the industrial proletariat and prevented the rise and development of crafts. As a result of this process there appeared among us as the main force in the towns, at the moment of the bourgeois revolution, an industrial proletariat of an extremely highly developed social type. This is a fact. It cannot be disputed, and must be taken as the basis of our revolutionary tactical conclusions.

'If the Menshevik comrades believe in the victory of the revolution, or even if they only recognize the possibility of such a victory, they cannot dispute the fact that in our country there is no historical claimant to revolutionary power other than the proletariat. As the petty bourgeois urban democracy in the Great French Revolution placed itself at the head of the revolutionary nation, in just the same way the proletariat, which is the one and only revolutionary democracy of our cities, must find a support in the peasant masses and place itself in power—if the revolution has any prospect of victory at all.

'*A government resting directly upon the proletariat, and through it upon the revolutionary peasantry, does not yet signify the socialist dictatorship.* I shall not here deal with the further prospects before a proletarian government. It may be that the proletariat is destined to fall, as did the Jacobin democracy, in order to clear the road for the rule of the bourgeoisie. I want to establish only one point: if the revolutionary movement in our country, as Plekhanov foretold, triumphs as a workers' movement, then the victory of the revolution is possible only as the revolutionary victory of the proletariat—otherwise it is altogether impossible.

'I insist upon this conclusion, most emphatically. If it is assumed that the social antagonisms between the proletariat and the peasant masses will prevent the proletariat from placing itself at the head of the latter, and that the proletariat by itself is not strong enough to gain victory—then one must necessarily draw the conclusion that there is no victory at all in store for our revolution. Under such circumstances, an agreement between the liberal bourgeoisie and the old authorities is bound to be the natural outcome of the revolution. This is a variant the possibility of which can by no means be denied. But clearly this variant lies along the path of the revolution's defeat, and is conditioned by its internal weakness. In essence *the entire analysis of the Mensheviks—above all, their evaluation, of the proletariat and its possible relations with the peasantry—leads them inexorably to the path of revolutionary pessimism.*

'But they persistently turn aside from this path and generate revolutionary optimism on the basis of—bourgeois democracy.

'From this is derived their attitude to the Cadets. For them the Cadets are the symbol of bourgeois democracy, while bourgeois democracy is the natural claimant to revolutionary power ...

'Upon what then do you base your belief that the Cadets will still rise and stand erect? Upon facts of political development? No, upon your own schema. In order "to early the revolution through to the end" you need the bourgeois urban democracy, you search for it eagerly, and find nothing but Cadets. And you generate in relation to them amazing optimism, you dress them up, you want to force them to play a creative role, a role which they do not want to play, cannot play and will not play. To my basic question—I have put it repeatedly—I have heard no response. You have no prognosis of the revolution. Your policy lacks any large prospects.

'And in connection with this, your attitude to bourgeois parties is formulated in words which the congress should keep in its memory: "as the occasion may require." The proletariat is not supposed to carry on a systematic struggle for influence over the masses of the people, it is not supposed to determine its tactical steps in accordance with a single guiding idea, namely, to unite around itself all the toilers and the downtrodden and to become their herald and leader. (*Minutes and Resolutions of the Fifth Party Congress.*)

This speech, which succinctly sums up all my articles, speeches and acts of 1905 and 1906, was completely approved by the Bolsheviks, not to mention Rosa Luxemburg and Tyszko (on the basis of this speech, we entered upon more intimate relations which led to my collaboration in the Polish journal). Lenin, who did not forgive me my conciliatory attitude toward the Mensheviks and he was right—expressed himself upon my speech with a deliberately emphasized reserve. Here is what he said:

'I merely wish to observe that Trotsky, in his little book *In Defence of the Party* publicly expressed his solidarity with Kautsky, who wrote of the economic community of interests of the proletariat and the peasantry in the present revolution in Russia. Trotsky recognized the admissibility and expediency of a left bloc against the liberal bourgeoisie. These facts are enough for me to recognize that Trotsky is drawing closer to our conceptions. *Independently of the question of the "uninterrupted revolution"*, there is solidarity here between us on the fundamental points of the question concerning the relationship to the bourgeois parties.

Lenin did not devote himself in his speech to a general evaluation of the theory of the permanent revolution, since I too, in my speech, did not develop the further prospects for the dictatorship of the proletariat. He had obviously not read my fundamental work on this question, otherwise he would not have spoken of my 'drawing closer' to the conceptions of the Bolsheviks as of something new, for my London speech was only a condensed restatement of my works of 1905-06. Lenin expressed himself very reservedly, because I did stand outside the Bolshevik faction. In spite of that, or more correctly, precisely because of that, his words leave no room for false interpretations. Lenin established 'solidarity between us on the fundamental points of the question' concerning the attitude toward the peasantry and the liberal bourgeoisie. This solidarity applies not to my *aims*, as Radek preposterously represents it, but precisely to *method*. As to the prospect of the democratic revolution growing into the socialist revolution, it is right here that Lenin makes the reservation, 'independently of the question of the "uninterrupted revolution".' What is the meaning of this reservation? It is clear that Lenin in no way identified the permanent revolution with ignoring the peasantry or skipping over the agrarian revolution, as is the rule with the ignorant and unscrupulous epigones. Lenin's idea is as follows: How far our revolution will go, whether the proletariat can come to power in our country sooner than in Europe and what prospects this opens up for socialism—this question I do not touch upon; however, on the fundamental question of the attitude of the proletariat toward the peasantry and the liberal bourgeoisie 'there is solidarity here between us.'

We have seen above how the Bolshevik *Novaya Zhizn* responded to the theory of the permanent revolution virtually at its birth, that is, as far back as in 1905. Let us also recall how the editors of Lenin's *Collected Works* expressed themselves on this theory after 1917. In the notes to Volume XIV, Part 2, it is stated:

'Even before the 1905 Revolution he (Trotsky) advanced the original and *now especially noteworthy* theory of the permanent revolution, in which he asserted that *the bourgeois revolution of 1905 would pass directly over into a socialist revolution*, constituting the first in a series of national revolutions.'

I grant that this is not at all an acknowledgement of the correctness of all that I have written on the permanent revolution. But in any case it is an acknowledgement of the incorrectness of what Radek writes about it. 'The *bourgeois* revolution will pass directly over into a socialist revolution'—but this is precisely the theory of *growing into* and not of *skipping over*; from this flows a realistic, and not an adventuristic tactic. And what is the meaning of the words *'now especially noteworthy* theory of the permanent revolution'? They mean that the October revolution has shed a new light on those aspects of the theory which had formerly remained in obscurity for many or had simply appeared 'improbable'. The second part of Volume XIV of Lenin's *Collected Works* appeared while the author was alive. Thousands and tens of thousands of party members read this note. And nobody declared it to be false until the year 1924. And it occurred to Radek to do this only in the year 1928.

But insofar as Radek speaks not only of theory but also of tactics, the most important argument against him still remains the character of my practical participation in the revolutions of 1905 and 1917. My work in the Petersburg Soviet of 1905 coincided with the definitive elaboration of those of my views on the nature of the revolution which the epigones now subject to uninterrupted fire. How could such allegedly erroneous views fail to be reflected in any way in my political activity, which was carried on before the eyes of everyone and recorded daily in the press? But if it is assumed that such a false theory was mirrored in my politics, then why did those who are now the consuls remain silent at that time? And what is rather more important, why did Lenin at that time most energetically defend the line of the Petersburg **Soviet**, at the highest point of the revolution as well as after its defeat?

The very same questions, only in a perhaps sharper form, apply to the 1917 revolution. In a number of articles which I wrote in New York, I evaluated the February Revolution from the point of view of the theory of the permanent revolution. Ah these articles have now been reprinted. My tactical conclusions coincided completely with the conclusions which Lenin drew at the same time in Geneva, and consequently were in the same irreconcilable contradiction to the conclusions of Kamenev, Stalin and the other epigones. When I arrived in Petrograd, nobody asked me if I renounced my 'errors' of the permanent revolution. Nor was there anyone to ask. Stalin slunk around in embarrassment from one corner to another and had only one desire that the party should forget as quickly as possible the policy which he had advocated up to Lenin's arrival. Yaroslavsky was not yet the inspirer of the Control Commission; together with Mensheviks, together with Ordzhonikidze and others, he was publishing a trivial semi-liberal sheet in Yakutsk. Kamenev accused Lenin of Trotskyism and declared when he met me: 'Now you have the laugh on us.' On the eve of the October Revolution, I wrote in the central organ of the Bolsheviks on the prospect of the permanent revolution. It never occurred to anyone to come out against me. My solidarity with Lenin turned out to be complete and unconditional. What then, do my critics, among them Radek, wish to say? That I myself completely failed to understand the theory which I advocated, and that in the most critical historical periods I acted directly counter to this theory, and quite correctly? Is it not simpler to assume that my critics failed to understand the permanent revolution, like so many other things? For if it is assumed that these belated critics are so well able to analyze not only their own ideas but those of others, then how explain that all of them without exception adopted such a wretched position in the 1917 Revolution, and forever covered themselves with shame in the Chinese Revolution?

But after all, some reader may suddenly recall: What about your most important tactical slogan; 'No Tsar-but a workers' government'?

In certain circles this argument is deemed decisive. Trotsky's horrid slogan, 'No Tsar! ' runs through all the writings of all the critics of the permanent revolution; with some it emerges as the final, most important and decisive argument; with others, as the ready harbour for weary minds.

This criticism naturally reaches its greatest profundity in the 'Master' of ignorance and disloyalty, when he says in his incomparable *Problems of Leninism* :

'We shall not dwell at length (No indeed!—L.T.) on Comrade Trotsky's attitude in 1905, when he 'simply' forgot all about the peasantry as a revolutionary force, and advanced the slogan of "No Tsar, but a workers' government", that is, the slogan of revolution without the peasantry.' (Stalin, *Problems of Leninism.*)

Despite my almost hopeless position in face of this annihilating criticism, which does not want to 'dwell', I should nevertheless like to refer to some mitigating circumstances. There are some. I beg a hearing.

Even if one of my 1905 articles contained an isolated, ambiguous or inappropriate slogan which might be open to misunderstanding, then today, i.e., 23 years later, it should not be taken by itself but rather placed in context with my other writings on the same subject, and, what is most important, in context with my political participation in the events. It is impermissible merely to provide readers with the bare title of a work unknown to them (as well as to the critics) and then to invest this title with a meaning which is diametrically opposed to everything I wrote and did.

But it may not be superfluous to add—O my critics!—that at no time and in no place did I ever write or utter or propose such a slogan as 'No Tsar—but a workers' government! At the basis of the main argument of my judges there lies, aside from everything else, a shameful factual error. The fact of the matter is that a proclamation entitled 'No Tsar—but a workers' government' was written and published abroad in the summer of 1905 by Parvus. I had already been living illegally for a long time in Petersburg at that period, and had nothing at all to do with this leaflet either in ideas or in actions. I learned of it much later from polemical articles. I never had the occasion or opportunity to express myself on it. As for the proclamation I (as also, moreover, all my critics) neither saw it nor read it. This is the factual side of this extraordinary affair. I am sorry that I must deprive all the Thaelmanns and Semards of this easily portable and convincing argument. But facts are stronger than my humane feelings.

Nor is this all. Accident providentially brought events together, so that, at the same time that Parvus was publishing abroad the circular, unknown to me, 'No Tsar—but a workers' government', a proclamation written by me appeared illegally in Petersburg with the title: *Neither Tsar nor Zemtsi, but the People!* This title, which is frequently repeated in the text of the leaflet as a slogan embracing the workers and peasants, might have been conceived in order to refute in a popular form the later contentions about skipping the democratic stage of the revolution. The appeal is reprinted in my *Collected Works* (Volume II, Part 1). There also are my proclamations, published by the Bolshevik Central Committee, to that peasantry, which, in the ingenious expression of Stalin, I 'simply forgot'.

But even this is not yet all. Only a short time ago, the worthy Rafes, a theoretician and leader of the Chinese Revolution, wrote in the theoretical organ of the Central Committee of the Communist Party of the Soviet Union about the same horrid slogan which Trotsky raised *in the year 1917*. Not in 1905, but in 1917! For the Menshevik Rafes, at any rate, there is some excuse—almost up till 1920 he was a 'minister' of Petlyura's, and how could he, weighed down by the cares of state of the struggle against the Bolsheviks, pay any heed there to what was going on in the camp of the October Revolution! Well, but the editorial board of the organ of the Central Committee? Here's a wonder. One idiocy more or less. ...

'But how is that possible?' a conscientious reader raised on the trash of recent years exclaims. 'Weren't we taught in hundreds and thousands of books and articles?'

'Yes, friends, taught: and that is just why you will have to learn anew. These are the overhead expenses of the period of reaction. Nothing can be done about it. History does not proceed in a straight line. It has temporarily run into Stalin's blind alleys.'

Notes

1. Do the belated critics of the permanent revolution agree with this? Are they prepared to extend this elementary proposition to the countries of the East, China, India, etc.? Yes or no?— L.T.

CHAPTER FIVE

WAS THE DEMOCRATIC DICTATORSHIP REALIZED IN OUR COUNTRY? IF SO, WHEN?

Appealing to Lenin, Radek contends that the democratic dictatorship was realized in the form of the dual power. Yes, *occasionally* -- and furthermore, conditionally—Lenin did put the question this way; that I admit. 'Occasionally?' Radek becomes indignant and accuses me of assailing one of the most fundamental ideas of Lenin. But Radek is angry only because he is wrong. In*Lessons of October*, which Radek likewise submits to criticism after a delay of about four years, I interpreted Lenin's words on the 'realization' of the democratic dictatorship in the following manner:

'A democratic workers' and peasants' coalition could only take shape as an immature form of power incapable of attaining <u>real power</u>—it could take shape only as a tendency and not as a concrete fact.' (*Collected Works*, Vol. III, part 1.)

With regard to this interpretation, Radek writes: 'Such an interpretation of the content of one of the most outstanding theoretical chapters in the work of Lenin *is worth absolutely nothing.*' These words are followed by a pathetic appeal to the traditions of Bolshevism, and finally, the conclusion: 'These questions are too important for it to be possible to reply to them with a reference to what Lenin *occasionally* said.'

By this, Radek wants to evoke the image of my treating carelessly 'one of the most outstanding' of Lenin's ideas. But Radek is wasting indignation and pathos for nothing. A little understanding would be more in place here. My presentation in *Lessons of October*,even though very condensed, does not rest upon a sudden inspiration on the basis of quotations taken at second hand, but upon a genuine thorough study of Lenin's writings. It reproduces the essence of Lenin's idea on this question, while the verbose presentation of Radek, despite the abundance of quotations, does not retain a single living passage of Lenin's thought.

Why did I make use of the qualifying word 'occasionally'? Because that is how the matter really stood. References to the fact that the democratic dictatorship was 'realized' in the form of the dual power ('in a certain form and up to a certain point') were made by Lenin only in the period between April and October 1917, that is, *before the actual carrying out of the democratic revolution.* Radek neither noticed, understood, nor evaluated this. In the struggle against the present epigones, Lenin spoke extremely conditionally of the 'realization' of the democratic dictatorship He did so not to give a historical characterization of the period of the dual power—in this form it would be plain nonsense—but to argue against those who expected a second, improved edition of the independent democratic dictatorship. Lenin's words only meant that there is not and will not be any democratic dictatorship outside of the miserable miscarriage of the dual power, and that for this reason it was necessary to 'rearm' the party, i.e., change the slogan. To contend that the coalition of the Mensheviks and the Socialist-Revolutionaries with the bourgeoisie, which refused the peasants the land and hounded the Bolsheviks, constituted the 'realization' of the Bolshevik slogan—this means either deliberately to pass off black as white or else to have lost one's head entirely.

With regard to the Mensheviks, an argument could be presented which would to a certain point be analogous to Lenin's argument against Kamenev: 'You are citing for the bourgeoisie to fulfill a "progressive" mission in the revolution? This mission has already been realized: the political role of Rodzianko, Guchkov and Milyukov is the maximum that the bourgeoisie is able to give, just as Kerenskyism is the maximum of democratic revolution that could be realized as an independent stage.'

Unmistakable anatomical features—rudiments—show that our ancestors had a tail. These features suffice to confirm the genetic unity of the animal world. But, to put it quite candidly, man has no tail. Lenin demonstrated to Kamenev the rudiments of the democratic dictatorship in the regime of the dual power, warning him that no new organ should be hoped for out of these rudiments. And we did not have an independent democratic dictatorship, even though we completed the democratic revolution more deeply, more resolutely, more purely than had ever been done anywhere else.

Radek should reflect upon the fact that if in the period from February to April the democratic dictatorship had *actually* been realized, even Molotov would have recognized it. The party and the class understood the democratic dictatorship as a regime which would mercilessly destroy the old state apparatus of the monarchy and completely liquidate manorial landed property. But there was not a trace of this in the Kerensky period. For the Bolshevik Party, however, it was a question of the *actual realization of the revolutionary tasks*, and not of the revelation of certain sociological and historical 'rudiments'. Lenin, in order to enlighten his adversaries theoretically, illuminated splendidly these features which did not attain development—and that is all he did in this connexion. Radek, however, endeavors in all seriousness to convince us that in the period of the dual power, that is, of powerlessness, the 'dictatorship' did exist and the democratic revolution was realized. Only, you see, it was such a 'democratic revolution' that all Lenin's genius was required to recognize it. But this is just the thing that signifies that it was not realized. The real democratic revolution is something that every illiterate peasant in Russia or in China would easily recognize. But so far as the morphological features are concerned, it is a more difficult thing. For example, despite the lesson provided by Kamenev in Russia, it is impossible to get Radek to finally take note of the fact that in China too the democratic dictatorship was likewise 'realized' in Lenin's sense (through the Kuomintang); and that it was realized more completely and in a more finished form than was the case in our country through the institution of dual power. Only hopeless simpletons can expect a second and improved edition of 'democracy' in China.

If the democratic dictatorship had only been realized in our country in the form of Kerenskyism, which played the role of errand boy to Lloyd George and Clemenceau, then we would have to say that history indulged in cruel mockery of the strategic slogan of Bolshevism. Fortunately, it is not so. The Bolshevik slogan was realized in fact—not as a morphological trait but as a very great historical reality. Only, it was realized *not before, but after October*. The peasant war, in the words of Marx, supported the dictatorship of the proletariat. The collaboration of the two classes was realized through October on a gigantic scale. At that time every ignorant peasant grasped and felt, even without Lenin's commentaries, that the Bolshevik slogan had been given life. And Lenin himself estimated the October Revolution—its first stage—as the *true* realization of the democratic revolution, and by that also as the true, even if changed, embodiment of the strategic slogan of the Bolsheviks. The *whole* of Lenin must be considered. And above all, the Lenin of after October, when he surveyed and evaluated events from a higher vantage point. Finally, Lenin must be considered in a Leninist way, and not in that of the epigones.

The question of the class character of the revolution and its 'growing over' was submitted by Lenin (after October) to an analysis in his book against Kautsky. Here is one of the passages over which Radek should reflect a bit.

'Yes, our revolution (the October Revolution—L.T.) is a bourgeois revolution *so long* as we march with the peasantry *as a whole*. This has been clear as clear can be to us; we have said it hundreds and thousands of times since 1905, and we have never attempted to skip this necessary stage of the historical process or abolish it by decrees.'

And further on:

'Things have turned out just as we said they would. The course taken by the revolution has confirmed the correctness of our reasoning. *First*, with the "whole" of the peasantry against the monarchy, the landlords, the mediaeval regime (and to that extent, the revolution remains bourgeois, bourgeois-democratic). Then with the poorest peasants, with the semi-proletarians, with all the exploited, *against capitalism*, including the rural rich, the kulaks, the profiteers, and to that extent the revolution becomes a *socialist* one.'

That is how Lenin spoke—not 'occasionally' but always, or, more accurately *invariably*—when he gave a finished and generalized and perfected evaluation of the revolution, including October. 'Things have turned out just as we said they would.' The bourgeois-democratic revolution was realized as a coalition of the workers and peasants. During the Kerensky period? No, *during the first period after October*. Is that right? It is. But, as we now know, it was not realized in the form of a democratic dictatorship, but in the form of the dictatorship of the proletariat. With that there also disappeared the necessity for the old algebraic formula.

If the conditional argument of Lenin against Kamenev in 1917 and the rounded-out Leninist characterization of the **October Revolution** in the subsequent years are uncritically juxtaposed, then it follows that two democratic revolutions were 'realized' in Russia. This is too much, all the more since the second is separated from the first by an armed uprising of the proletariat.

Now contrast the quotation just made from Lenin's book, *The Proletarian Revolution and the Renegade Kautsky*, with the passage from my *Results and Prospects* where, in the chapter on 'The Proletarian Regime', the first stage of the dictatorship and the prospects of its further development are outlined:

'The abolition of feudalism will meet with support from the *entire* peasantry as the burden-bearing estate. A progressive income tax will also be supported by the great majority of the peasantry. But any legislation carried through for the purpose of protecting the agricultural proletariat will not only not receive the active sympathy of the majority, but will even meet with the active opposition of a minority of the peasantry. The proletariat will find itself compelled to carry the class struggle into the villages and in this manner destroy the community of interest which is undoubtedly to be found among all peasants, although within comparatively narrow limits. From the very first moment after its taking power, the proletariat will have to find support in the antagonisms between the village poor and the village rich, between the agricultural proletariat and the agricultural bourgeoisie.' (*Our Revolution*, 1906.)

How little all this resembles an 'ignoring' of the peasantry on my part, and the complete 'antagonism' between the two lines, Lenin's and mine!

The quotation from Lenin adduced above does not stand alone in his works. On the contrary, as is always the case with Lenin, the new formula, which illuminates events more penetratingly, becomes for him the axis of his speeches and his articles for a whole period. In March 1919, Lenin said:

'In October 1917 we seized power *together with the peasantry as a whole*. This was a bourgeois revolution, inasmuch as the class struggle in the rural districts had not yet developed.'

The following was said by Lenin at the party congress in March 1919:

'In a country where the proletariat was obliged to assume power with the aid of the peasantry, where it fell to the lot of the proletariat to serve as the agent of a petty-bourgeois revolution, until the organization of the Committees of Poor Peasants, i.e., down to the summer and even the autumn of 1918, our revolution was to a large extent a *bourgeois* revolution.'

These words were frequently repeated by Lenin in different variations and on divers occasions. Radek, however, simply avoids this cardinal idea of Lenin's, which is decisive in the controversy.

The proletariat took power together with the peasantry in October, says Lenin. By that alone, the revolution was a bourgeois revolution. Is that right? In a certain sense, yes. But this means that the *true* democratic dictatorship of the proletariat and the peasantry, that is, the one which actually destroyed the regime of autocracy and serfdom and snatched the land from the feudalists, was accomplished not *before* October but only *after* October; it was accomplished, to use Marx's words, in the form of the *dictatorship of the proletariat supported by the peasant war*—and then, a few months later, began growing into a socialist dictatorship. Is this really hard to understand? Can differences of opinion prevail on this point *today*?

According to Radek, the 'permanent' theory sins by mixing up the bourgeois stage with the socialist. In reality, however, the class dynamics so thoroughly 'mixed up', that is, *combined* these two stages, that our unfortunate metaphysician is no longer in a position even to find the threads.

Certainly, many gaps and many incorrect contentions can be found in *Results and Prospects*. But after all, this work was written not in 1928, but considerably before October—before the October of 1905. The question of the gaps in the theory of the permanent revolution, or, more correctly, in my basic arguments for this theory at that time, is not even touched upon by Radek; for, following his teachers—the epigones—he attacks not the gaps but the strong sides of the theory, those which the course of historical development confirmed, attacks them in the name of the utterly false conclusions which he deduces from Lenin's formulation—which Radek has not thoroughly studied or thought out to the very end.

Juggling with old quotations is in general practiced by the whole school of epigones on a quite special plane which nowhere intersects the real historical process. But when the opponents of 'Trotskyism' have to occupy themselves with the analysis of the real development of the October Revolution, and occupy themselves with it seriously and conscientiously—which happens to some of them from time to time— then they inevitably arrive at formulations in the spirit of the theory which they reject. We find the dearest proof of this in the works of A. Yakovlev which are devoted to the history of the October Revolution. The class relationships of old Russia are formulated by this author, today a prop of the ruling faction and undoubtedly more literate than the other Stalinists, and particularly than Stalin himself, as follows :

'We see a twofold limitedness in the peasants' uprising (March to October 1917). Raising itself to the level of a peasant war, the uprising did not overcome its limitedness, did not burst asunder the confines of its immediate task of destroying the neighboring landowner; did not transform itself into an organized revolutionary movement; did not surmount the character of an elemental outbreak that distinguishes a peasant movement.

'The peasant uprising taken by itself—an elemental uprising, limited in its aim to the extermination of the neighboring landowner—could not triumph, could not destroy the state power hostile to the peasantry, which supported the landowner. That is why the agrarian movement is capable of winning only if it is led by the corresponding urban class ... This is the reason why the fate of the agrarian revolution, in the final analysis, was decided not in the tens of thousands of villages, but in the hundreds of towns. Only the working class, which was dealing the bourgeoisie a mortal blow in the centers of the country, could bring the peasant uprising to victory; only the victory of the working class in the city could tear the peasant movement out of the confines of an elemental clash of tens of millions of peasants with tens of thousands of landowners; only the victory of the working class, finally, could lay the foundations for a new type of peasant organization which united the poor and middle peasantry not with the bourgeoisie but with the working class. The problem of the victory of the peasant uprising was a problem of the victory of the working class in the towns.

'When the workers dealt the government of the bourgeoisie a decisive blow in October, they thereby solved in passing the problem of the victory of the peasant uprising.'

And further on:

'. . . The whole essence of the matter is this, that by virtue of the historically given conditions, bourgeois Russia in 1917 entered into an alliance with the landowners. Even the most left factions of the bourgeoisie, like the Mensheviks and the Socialist-Revolutionaries, did not go beyond arranging a deal favorable to the landowners. Therein lies the most important difference between the conditions of the Russian Revolution and the French Revolution which took place more than a hundred years earlier ... The peasant revolution could not triumph as a bourgeois revolution in 1917. (Exactly !—L.T.) Two roads were open to it. *Either defeat under the blows of the bourgeoisie and the landowners or—victory as movement accompanying and auxiliary to the proletarian revolution. By taking over the mission of the bourgeoisie in the Great French Revolution, by taking over the task of leading the agrarian democratic revolution, the working class of Russia obtained the possibility of carrying out a victorious proletarian revolution.' (The Peasant Movement in 1917*, State Publishing House, 1927).

What are the fundamental elements of Yakovlev's arguments? The incapacity of the peasantry to play an *independent* political role: the resultant inevitability of the leading role of an urban class; the inaccessibility for the Russian bourgeoisie of the role of leader in the agrarian revolution; the resultant inevitability of the leading role of the proletariat; its seizure of power as leader of the agrarian revolution; finally, the dictatorship of the proletariat which supports itself upon the peasant war and opens up the epoch of socialist revolution. This destroys to the roots the metaphysical posing of the question concerning the 'bourgeois' or the 'socialist' character of the revolution. The gist of the matter lay in the fact that the agrarian question, which constituted the basis of the bourgeois revolution, could not be solved under the rule of the bourgeoisie. The dictatorship of the proletariat appeared on the scene not after the completion of the agrarian democratic revolution but as the necessary *prerequisite* for its accomplishment. In a word, in this retrospective schema of Yakovlev's, we have all the fundamental elements of the theory of the permanent revolution as formulated by me in 1905. With me, it was a question of a historical prognosis; Yakovlev, relying upon the preliminary studies of a whole staff of young research workers, draws the balance sheet of the events of the three revolutions twenty-two years after the first revolution and ten years after the October Revolution. And then? Yakovlev repeats almost literally my formulations of 1905.

What is Yakovlev's attitude, however, to the theory of the permanent revolution? It is an attitude that befits every Stalinist functionary who wants to retain his post and even to climb to a higher one. But how does Yakovlev, in this case, reconcile his appraisal of the driving forces of the October Revolution with the struggle against 'Trotskyism'? Very simply: he does not give a thought to such reconciliation. Like some liberal Tsarist officials, who acknowledged Darwin's theory but at the same time appeared regularly at communion, Yakovlev too buys the right to express Marxist ideas from time to time at the price of participating in the ritualistic baiting of the permanent revolution. Similar examples can be adduced by the dozen.

It still remains to add that Yakovlev did not execute the above-quoted work on the history of the October Revolution on his own initiative, but on the basis of a decision of the Central Committee, which at the same time charged me with the editing of Yakovlev's work.[1] At that time, Lenin's recovery was still expected, and it never occurred to any of the epigones to kindle an artificial dispute around the permanent revolution. At any rate, in my capacity as the former, or, more correctly, as the proposed editor of the official history of the October Revolution, I can establish with complete satisfaction that the author, in all disputed questions, consciously or unconsciously employed the literal formulations of my proscribed and heretical work on the permanent revolution (*Results and Prospects*).

The rounded-out evaluation of the historical fate of the Bolshevik slogan which Lenin himself gave shows with certainty that the difference of the two lines, the 'permanent' and Lenin's, had a secondary and subordinate significance; what united them, however, was most fundamental. And this foundation of both lines, which were completely fused by the October Revolution, is in irreconcilable antagonism not only to the February-March line of Stalin and the April-October line of Kamenev, Rykov and Zinoviev, not only to the whole China policy of Stalin, Bukharin and Martynov, but also to the present 'China' line of Radek.

And when Radek, who changed his judgment of values so radically between 1925 and the second half of 1928, seeks to convict me of not understanding: 'the complexity of Marxism and Leninism', then I can reply: The *fundamental* train of thought which I developed twenty-three years ago in *Results and Prospects*, I consider confirmed by events as completely correct, and, precisely because of that, in agreement with the strategic line of Bolshevism.

In particular I fail to see the slightest reason for withdrawing anything of what I said in 1922 on the permanent revolution in the foreword to my book *The Year 1905*, which the whole party read and studied in innumerable editions and reprints while Lenin was alive, and which 'disturbed' Kamenev only in the autumn of 1924 and Radek for the first time in the autumn of 1928.

'Precisely in the period between January 9 and the October strike' (it says in this foreword) 'the author formed those opinions which later received the name: "theory of the permanent revolution". This somewhat unusual name expressed the idea that the Russian revolution, directly confronted by bourgeois tasks, could in no case halt at them. *The revolution would not be able to solve its immediate bourgeois tasks except by putting the proletariat in power ...*

'This appraisal was confirmed as completely correct, though after a lapse of twelve years. The Russian revolution could not terminate with a bourgeois-democratic regime. It had to transfer power to the working class. *If the working class was still too weak for the capture of power in 1905, it had to mature and grow strong not in the bourgeois-democratic republic but in the illegality of Third-of-June Tsarism.'* (L. Trotsky *The Year 1905*, foreword).

I want to quote in addition one of the sharpest polemical judgments which I passed on the slogan of the 'democratic dictatorship'. In 1909, I wrote in the Polish organ of Rosa Luxemburg:

'While the Mensheviks, proceeding from the abstraction that "our revolution is bourgeois" arrive at the idea of adapting the whole tactic of the proletariat to the conduct of the liberal bourgeoisie, right up to the capture of state power, the Bolsheviks, proceeding from the same bare abstraction: "democratic, not socialist dictatorship", arrive at the idea of the bourgeois-democratic self-limitation of the proletariat with power in its hands. The difference between them on this question is certainly quite important: while the anti-revolutionary sides of Menshevism are already expressed in full force today, the anti-revolutionary features of Bolshevism threaten to become a great danger only in the event of the victory of the revolution.'

To this passage in the article, which is reprinted in the Russian edition of my book *The Year 1905*, I made the following annotation in January 1922:

'As is known, this did not take place, for Bolshevism under the leadership of Lenin (though not without internal struggle), accomplished its ideological rearmament on this most important question in the spring of 1917, that is, before the seizure of power.'

These two quotations have been subjected since 1924 to a furious barrage of criticism. Now, after a delay of four years, Radek has also joined in with this criticism. Yet, if one reflects conscientiously upon the quoted lines, it must be admitted that they contained an important prognosis and a no less important warning. The fact does remain that at the moment of the February Revolution the whole so-called 'old guard' of the Bolsheviks held the position of the bald counter-posing of the democratic dictatorship to the socialist dictatorship. Out of Lenin's 'algebraic 'formula his closest disciples made a purely metaphysical construction and directed it against the real development of the revolution. At a most important historical turning point, the top leadership of the Bolsheviks in Russia adopted a reactionary position, and had Lenin not arrived so opportunely they could have knifed the October Revolution under the banner of the struggle against Trotskyism, as they later knifed the Chinese Revolution. Very piously, Radek describes the false position of the whole leading party stratum as a sort of 'accident'. But that has little value as a Marxist explanation of the vulgar democratic position of Kamenev, Zinoviev, Stalin, Molotov, Rykov, Kalinin, Nogin, Milyutin, Krestlusky, Frunze, Yaroslavsky, Ordjonikidze, Preobrazhensky, Smilga and a dozen other 'old Bolsheviks'.

Would it not be more correct to acknowledge that the old, algebraic Bolshevik formula contained certain dangers within it? Political development filled it -- as always happens with an ambiguous revolutionary formula—with a content hostile to the proletarian revolution. It is self-evident that if Lenin had lived in Russia and had observed the development of the party, day by day, especially during the war, he would have given the necessary correctives and clarifications in time. Luckily for the revolution, he arrived soon enough, even though delayed, to undertake the necessary ideological rearmament. The class instinct of the proletariat and the revolutionary pressure of the party rank and file, prepared by the entire preceding work of Bolshevism, made it possible for Lenin, in struggle with the top leadership and despite their resistance, to switch tire policy of the party to a new track in ample time.

Does it really follow from this that today we must accept for China, India and other countries Lenin's formula of 1905 in its algebraic form, i.e., in all its ambiguity; and that we must leave it to the Chinese and Indian Stalins and Rykovs (Tang Ping-shan, Roy and others) to fill the formula with a petty-bourgeois national-democratic content—and then wait for the timely appearance of a Lenin who will undertake the necessary correctives of April 4? But is such a corrective assured for China and India? Wouldn't it be more appropriate to introduce into this formula those specific corrections the necessity for which has been demonstrated by historical experience both in Russia and in China?

Does the foregoing mean that the slogan of the democratic dictatorship of the proletariat and peasantry should be understood simply as a 'mistake'? Nowadays, as we know, all ideas and actions of man are divided into two categories: absolutely correct ones, that is, those that comprise the 'general line', and absolutely false ones, that is, deviations from this line. This, of course, does not prevent what is absolutely correct today from being declared absolutely false tomorrow. But the real development of ideas knew also, before the emergence of the 'general line', the method of successive approximations to the truth. Even in simple division in arithmetic it is necessary to experiment in the selection of digits; one starts with larger or smaller digits, and then rejects ah but one in the process of testing. In ranging the target in artillery fire, the method of successive approximations is known as 'bracketing'. There is absolutely no avoiding the method of approximation in politics as well. The whole point is to understand in time that a miss is a miss, and to introduce the necessary corrections without delay.

The great historic significance of Lenin's formula lay in the fact that, under the conditions of a new historical epoch, it probed to the end one of the most important theoretical and political questions, namely the question of the degree of political independence attainable by the various petty-bourgeois groupings, above all, the peasantry. Thanks to its completeness, the Bolshevik experience of 1905-17 firmly bolted the door against the 'democratic dictatorship'. With his own hand, Lenin wrote the inscription over this door: No Entrance—No Exit. He formulated it in these words: The peasant must go either with the bourgeois or with the worker. The epigones, however, completely ignore this conclusion to which the old formula of Bolshevism led, and contrary to this conclusion they canonize a provisional hypothesis by inserting it into the program. It is really in this, generally speaking, that the essence of epigonism lies.

Notes

1. Excerpt from the minutes of the session of the Organization Bureau of the Central Committee of May 22, 1922, No. 21 : 'To instruct Comrade Yakovlev ... to compile a textbook on the history of the October Revolution under the editorial supervision of Comrade Trotsky.'—L.T.

CHAPTER SIX

ON THE SKIPPING OF HISTORICAL STAGES

Radek does not simply repeat a few of the official critical exercises of recent years, he also sometimes simplifies them, if that be possible. From what he writes, it follows that I make no distinction at all between the bourgeois and the socialist revolutions, between the East and the West, either in 1905 or today. Following Stalin, Radek too enlightens me on the impermissibility of skipping historical stages.

The question must be put first and foremost: If in 1905 it was for me simply a matter of the "socialist revolution" then why did I believe that it could begin in backward Russia sooner than in advanced Europe? Out of patriotism? Out of national pride? And yet, somehow, that is what did happen. Does Radek understand that if the democratic revolution had been realized in Russia as an *independent* stage, we should not have had today the dictatorship of the proletariat? If this came earlier here than in the West, then it was precisely and only because history combined the main content of the bourgeois revolution with the first stage of the proletarian revolution—did not mix them up but combined them organically.

To distinguish between the bourgeois and the proletarian revolution is political A.B.C. But after the A.B.C. come syllables, that is, combinations of letters. History accomplished just such a combination of the most important letters of the bourgeois alphabet with the first letters of the socialist alphabet. Radek, however, would like to drag us back from the already accomplished syllables to the alphabet. This is sad, but true.

It is nonsense to say that stages cannot in general be skipped. The living historical process always makes leaps over isolated "stages" which derive from theoretical breakdown into its component parts of the process of development in its entirety, that is, taken in its fullest scope. The same is demanded of revolutionary policy at critical moments. It may be said that the first distinction between a revolutionist and a vulgar evolutionist lies in the capacity to recognize and exploit such moments.

Marx's breakdown of the development of industry into handicraft, manufacture and factory is part of the A.B.C. of political economy, or more precisely, of historico-economic theory. In Russia, however, the factory came by skipping over the epoch of manufacture and of urban handicrafts. This is already among the syllables of history. An analogous process took place in our country in class relationships and in politics. The modern history of Russia cannot be comprehended unless the Marxist schema of the three stages is known: handicraft, manufacture and factory. But if one knows *only* this, one still comprehends nothing. For the fact is that the history of Russia—Stalin should not take this personally—skipped a few stages. The theoretical distinction of the stages, however, is necessary for Russia, too, otherwise one can comprehend neither what this leap amounted to nor what its consequences were.

The matter can also be approached from another side (just as Lenin occasionally approached the dual power), and it can be said that Russia went through all three of Marx's stages—the first two, however, in an extremely telescoped, embryonic form. These "rudiments", the stages of handicraft and manufacture—merely outlined in dots, so to speak—suffice to confirm the genetic unity of the economic process. Nevertheless, the quantitative contraction of the two stages was so great that it engendered an entirely new quality in the whole social structure of the nation. The most striking expression of this new "quality" in politics is the October Revolution.

What is most unbearable in this discussion is the "theorizing" of Stalin, with the two trinkets which constitute his entire theoretical baggage: "the law of uneven development" and the "non-skipping of stages". Stalin does not understand to this day that the *skipping of stages* (or remaining too long at one stage) *is just what uneven development consists of.* Against the theory of the permanent revolution, Stalin, with inimitable seriousness, sets up the law of uneven development. Yet, the prediction that historically backward Russia could arrive at the proletarian revolution sooner than advanced Britain rests entirely upon the law of uneven development. However, to make this prediction one had to understand the historical unevenness in its whole dynamic concreteness, and not simply keep permanently chewing upon a 1915 quotation from Lenin, which is turned upside down and interpreted in the manner of an illiterate.

The dialectic of the historical "stages" is relatively easy to understand in periods of revolutionary ascent. Reactionary periods, on the contrary, naturally become epochs of cheap evolutionism. Stalinism, this gross ideological vulgarity, the worthy daughter of the party reaction, has created a cult of its own of progress by stages, as a cover for its political tailism and haggling over rags. This reactionary ideology has now engulfed Radek too.

One stage or another of the historical process can prove to be inevitable under certain conditions, although theoretically not inevitable. And conversely, theoretically "inevitable" stages can be compressed to zero by the dynamics of development, especially during revolutions, which have not for nothing been called the locomotives of history.

For example, in our country the proletariat "skipped" the stage of democratic parliamentarianism, granting the Constituent Assembly only a few hours, and even that much only in the back yard. But the counter-revolutionary stage in China can in no way be skipped over, just as in Russia the period of the four Dumas could not be skipped over. The present counter-revolutionary stage in China, however, was historically in no sense "unavoidable". It is the direct result of the catastrophic policy of Stalin and Bukharin, who will pass into history as the organizers of defeats. But the fruits of opportunism have become an objective factor which can check the revolutionary process for a long time.

Every attempt to skip over real, that is, objectively conditioned stages in the development of the masses, is political adventurism. So long as the majority of the working masses have confidence in the Social Democrats, or let us say, the Kuomintang, or the trade union leaders, we cannot pose before them the task of the immediate overthrow of bourgeois power. The masses must be prepared for that. The preparation can prove to be a very long "stage". But only a tailist can believe that, "together with the masses", we must sit, first in the Right and then in the Left Kuomintang, or maintain a bloc with the strike-breaker Purcell "until the masses become disillusioned with their leaders"—whom we, in the meantime, uphold with our friendship.

Radek will hardly have forgotten that many "dialecticians" characterized the demand for withdrawal from the **Kuomintang** and the break with the Anglo-Russian Committee as nothing but a skipping over of stages, and besides that, as a breach with the peasantry (in China) and with the working masses (in Britain). Radek ought to remember this all the better since he himself was one of the "dialecticians" of this sorry type. Now he is merely deepening and generalizing his opportunist errors.

In April 1919, Lenin wrote in a programmatic article, "The Third International and Its Place in History":

"We should not be mistaken if we say that it is precisely this contradiction between the backwardness of Russia and its "leap" to the higher form of democracy, its leap across bourgeois democracy to Soviet, or proletarian democracy, that it was precisely this contradiction that was one of the reasons. . . which, in the West, particularly hindered, or retarded, the understanding of the role of the **Soviets**".

Lenin says here directly that Russia made a "leap across bourgeois democracy". To be sure, implicit in Lenin's statement are all the necessary qualifications: after all, the dialectic does not consist of each time repeating all the concrete conditions; the writer takes it for granted that the reader himself also has something in his head. The leap across bourgeois democracy remains in spite of that, and makes difficult, according to Lenin's correct observation, the understanding of the role of the Soviets by all dogmatists and schematists—not only "in the West", but also in the East.

And here is how this question is dealt with in the foreword to *The Year 1905*, which now suddenly causes Radek such disquiet:

"Already in 1905, the Petersburg workers called their **Soviet** a proletariat government. This designation passed into the everyday language of that time and was completely embodied in the program of the struggle of the working class for power. At the same time, however, *we set up against Tsarism an elaborated programme of political democracy* (universal suffrage, republic, militia, etc.). We could act in no other way. Political *democracy is a necessary stage in the development of the working masses* — with the highly important reservation that in one case this stage lasts for decades, while in another, the revolutionary situation permits the masses to emancipate themselves from the prejudices of political democracy even before its institutions have been converted into reality." (Trotsky, *The Year 1905*, foreword.)

These words, which, by the way, are in complete accord with the ideas of Lenin quoted by me above, sufficiently explain, I think, the necessity of setting up against the dictatorship of the Kuomintang an "elaborated program of political democracy". But it is precisely at this point that Radek swings to the left. In the epoch of the revolutionary ascent he opposed the withdrawal of the Chinese Communist Party from the Kuomintang. In the epoch of the counter-revolutionary dictatorship he resists the mobilization of the Chinese workers under democratic slogans. This amounts to wearing furs in summer and going naked in winter.

CHAPTER SEVEN

WHAT DOES THE SLOGAN OF THE DEMOCRATIC DICTATORSHIP MEAN TODAY FOR THE EAST

Losing his way in the Stalinist—evolutionary, philistine, and not revolutionary—conception of historical 'stages', Radek, too, endeavors now to sanctify the slogan of the democratic dictatorship of the proletariat and the peasantry for the whole East. Out of the 'working hypothesis' of Bolshevism, which Lenin adapted to the course of development of a specific country; which he changed, concretized and at a certain stage cast aside—Radek constructs a supra-historical schema. On this point he persistently repeats the following in his articles:

'This theory, as well as the tactic derived from it, is applicable to all countries with a youthful capitalist development, in which the bourgeoisie has not liquidated the problem that the preceding social-political formations have left behind as a heritage.'

Just reflect upon this formula: Is it not a solemn justification of Kamenev's position in 1917? Did the Russian bourgeoisie 'liquidate' the problems of the democratic revolution after the February Revolution? No, they remained unsolved, including the most important of them, the agrarian problem. How could Lenin fail to comprehend that the old slogan was still 'applicable'? Why did he withdraw it?

Radek answered us on this point before: because it had already 'been accomplished'. We have examined this answer. It is completely untenable, and doubly untenable in the mouth of Radek, who holds the view that the essence of the old Leninist slogan does not at all lie in the forms of power but in the actual liquidation of serfdom by the collaboration of the proletariat and the peasantry. But this is precisely what Kerenskyism did not produce. From this it follows that Radek's excursion into our past for the purpose of solving the most acute question of the day, the Chinese question, is altogether absurd. It is not what Trotsky understood or failed to understand in 1905 that should have been investigated, but rather what Stalin, Molotov and especially Rykov and Kamenev did not grasp in February-March 1917 (what Radek's position was in those days I do not know). For if one believes that the democratic dictatorship was 'realized' to such an extent in the dual power as to require an immediate change of the central slogan, then one must recognize that the 'democratic dictatorship' in China was realized much more fully and completely through the regime of the Kuomintang, that is, through the rule of Chiang Kai-shek and Wang Ching-wei, with Tang Ping-shan as appendage.[1] It was all the more necessary, therefore, to change the slogan in China.

But after all, is the 'heritage of the preceding social-political formations' not yet liquidated in China? No, it is not yet liquidated. But was it liquidated in Russia on April 4, 1917, when Lenin declared war upon the whole upper stratum of the 'old Bolsheviks'? Radek contradicts himself hopelessly, gets muddled and reels from side to side. Let us remark in this connection that it is not entirely accidental that he uses so complicated an expression as 'heritage of the formations', plays variations upon it, and obviously avoids the clearer term, 'remnants of feudalism or of serfdom', why? Because Radek only yesterday denied these remnants most decisively and thereby tore away any basis for the slogan of the democratic dictatorship. In his report in the Communist Academy, Radek said:

'The sources of the Chinese Revolution are no less deep than were the sources of our revolution in 1905. One can assert with certainty that the alliance of the working class with the peasantry will be stronger there than it was with us in 1905, *for the simple reason that it will not be directed against two classes, but only against one, the bourgeoisie.*'

Yes, 'for the simple reason'. What, when the proletariat, together with the peasantry, directs its fight against one class, the bourgeoisie -- not against the remnants of feudalism, but against the bourgeoisie—what, if you please, is such a revolution called ? Perhaps a democratic revolution? Just notice that Radek said this not in 1905, and not even in 1909, but in March 1927. How is this to be understood? Very simply. In March 1927, Radek also deviated from the right road, only in another direction. In its theses on the Chinese question, the Opposition inserted a most important correction to Radek's one-sidedness of that time. But in the words just quoted there was nevertheless a kernel of truth : there is almost no estate of landlords in China, the landowners are much more intimately bound up with the capitalists than in Tsarist Russia, and the specific weight of the agrarian question in China is therefore much lighter than in Tsarist Russia; but on the other hand, the question of national liberation bulks very large. Accordingly, the capacity of the Chinese peasantry for *independent* revolutionary political struggle for the democratic renovation of the country certainly cannot be greater than was the Russian peasantry's. This found its expression, among other things, in the bet that neither before 1925 nor during the three years of the revolution in China, did a Narodnik (Populist) party arise, inscribing the agrarian revolution upon its banner. All this taken together demonstrates that for China, which has already left behind it the experience of 1925-27, the formula of the democratic dictatorship presents a much more dangerous reactionary snare than in Russia after the February Revolution.

Still another excursion by Radek, into an even further distant past, turns just as mercilessly against him. This time, it is the matter of the slogan of the permanent revolution which Marx raised in 1850:

'With Marx.' writes Radek, 'there was no slogan of a democratic dictatorship, while with Lenin, from 1905 to 1917, it was the political axis, and formed a component part of his conception of the revolution *in all [? !] countries* of incipient [?] capitalist development.'

Basing himself upon a few lines from Lenin, Radek explains this difference of positions by the fact that the central task of the German revolution was *national unification*, while in Russia it was the *agrarian revolution*. If this contrast is not made mechanically, and a sense of proportion is maintained, then it is correct up to a certain point. But then how does the matter stand with China? The specific weight of the national problem in China, a semi-colonial country, is immeasurably greater in comparison with the agrarian problem than it was even in Germany in 1848-50; for in China it is simultaneously a question of unification and of liberation. Marx formulated his perspectives of the permanent revolution when, in Germany, all the thrones still stood firm, the Junkers held the land, and the leaders of the bourgeoisie were tolerated only in the antechamber of the government. In China, there has been no monarchy since 1911, there is no independent landlord class, the national-bourgeois Kuomintang is in power, and the relationships of serfdom are, so to speak, chemically fused with bourgeois exploitation. The contrast between the positions of Marx and Lenin undertaken by Radek thus tells entirely against the slogan of the democratic dictatorship in China.

But Radek does not even take up the position of Marx seriously, but only casually, episodically, confining himself to the circular of 1850, *in which Marx still considered the peasantry the natural ally of the petty-bourgeois urban democracy*. Marx at that time expected an independent stage of democratic revolution in Germany, that is, a temporary assumption of power by the urban petty-bourgeois radicals, supported by the peasantry. There's the nub of the question! That, however, is just what did not happen. And not by chance, either. Already in the middle of the last century, the petty-bourgeois democracy showed itself to be powerless to carry out its own independent revolution. And Marx took account of this lesson. On April 16, 1856—that is, six years after the circular mentioned—Marx wrote to Engels:

'The whole thing in Germany will depend on the possibility of covering the rear of the proletarian revolution by a second edition of the Peasants' War. Then the affair will be splendid.'

These remarkable words, completely forgotten by Radek, constitute a truly precious key to the October Revolution as well as to the whole problem that occupies us here, in its entirety. Did Marx skip over the agrarian Revolution? No, as we see, he did not skip over it. Did he consider the collaboration of the proletariat and the peasantry necessary in the coming revolution? Yes, he did. Did he grant the possibility of the leading, or even only an independent, role being played by the peasantry in the revolution? No, he did not grant this possibility. He proceeded from the fact that the peasantry, which had not succeeded in supporting the bourgeois democracy in the independent democratic revolution (through the fault of the bourgeois democracy, not of the peasantry), would be in a position to support the proletariat in the proletarian revolution. 'Then the affair will be splendid.' Radek apparently does not want to see that this is exactly what happened in October, and did not happen badly at that.

With regard to China, the conclusions following from this are quite clear. The dispute is not over the decisive role of the peasantry as an ally, and not over the great significance of the agrarian revolution, but over whether an independent agrarian democratic revolution is possible in China or whether 'a second edition of the Peasants' War' will give support to the proletarian dictatorship. That is the only way the question stands. Whoever puts it differently has learned nothing and understood nothing, but only confuses the Chinese Communist Party and puts it off the right track.

In order that the proletariat of the Eastern countries may open the road to victory, the pedantic reactionary theory of Stalin and Martynov on 'stages' and 'steps' must be eliminated at the very outset, must be cast aside, broken up and swept away with a broom. Bolshevism grew to maturity in the struggle against this vulgar evolutionism. It is not to a line of march marked out *a priori* that we must adapt ourselves, but to the real course of the class struggle. It is necessary to reject the idea of Stalin and Kuusinen—the idea of fixing an order of succession for countries at various levels of development by assigning them in advance cards for different rations of revolution. One must adapt oneself to the real course of the class struggle. An inestimable guide for this is Lenin; but the *whole* of Lenin must be taken into consideration.

When in 1919 Lenin, especially in connection with the organization of the Communist International, unified the conclusions of the period that had gone by, and gave them an ever more finished theoretical formulation, he interpreted the experience of Kerenskyism and October as follows: In a bourgeois society with already developed class antagonisms there can only be either the dictatorship of the bourgeoisie, open or disguised, or the dictatorship of the proletariat. There cannot be any talk of an intermediate regime. Every democracy, every 'dictatorship of democracy ' (the ironical quotation marks are Lenin's) is only a veil for the rule of the bourgeoisie, as the experience of the most backward European country, Russia, showed in the epoch of its bourgeois revolution, i.e., the epoch most favorable to the 'dictatorship of democracy'. This conclusion was taken by Lenin as the basis for his theses on democracy, which were produced only as the sum of the experiences of the February and October Revolutions.

Like many others, Radek also separates mechanically the question of democracy from the question of the democratic dictatorship. This is the source of the greatest blunders. The 'democratic dictatorship' can only be the masked rule of the bourgeoisie during the revolution. This is taught us by the experience of our 'dual power' of 1917 as well as by the experience of the Kuomintang in China.

The hopelessness of the epigones is most crassly expressed in the fact that even now they still attempt to contrast the democratic dictatorship to the dictatorship of the bourgeoisie, as well as to the dictatorship of the proletariat. But this means that the democratic dictatorship must be of an intermediate character, that is, have petty-bourgeois content. The participation of the proletariat in it does not alter matters, for in nature there is no such thing as an arithmetical mean of the various class lines. If it is neither the dictatorship of the bourgeoisie nor the dictatorship of the proletariat, then it follows that the petty-bourgeoisie must play the *determining* and *decisive* role. But this brings us back to the very same question which has been answered in practice by the three Russian and the two Chinese revolutions; is the petty-bourgeoisie today, under the conditions of the world domination of imperialism, capable of playing a leading revolutionary role in capitalist countries, even when it is a question of backward countries which are still confronted with the solution of their democratic tasks?

There have been epochs in which the lower strata of the petty-bourgeoisie were able to set up their revolutionary dictatorship. That we know. But those were epochs in which the proletariat or precursor of the proletariat, of the time had not yet become differentiated from the petty-bourgeoisie, but on the contrary constituted in its undeveloped condition the fighting core of the latter. It is quite otherwise today. We cannot speak of the ability of the petty-bourgeoisie to direct the life of present-day, even if backward, bourgeois society, insofar as the proletariat has already separated itself off from the petty-bourgeoisie and is pitted antagonistically against the big bourgeoisie on the basis of capitalist development, which condemns the petty-bourgeoisie to nullity and confronts the peasantry with the inevitable political choice between the bourgeoisie and the proletariat. Every time the peasantry decides for a party which on the surface seems petty-bourgeois, it actually offers its back as a support for finance capital. While in the period of the first Russian Revolution, or in the period between the first two revolutions, there could still exist differences of opinion over the *degree of independence* (but only the degree!) of the peasantry and the petty-bourgeoisie in the democratic revolution, now this question has been decided by the whole course of events of the last twelve years, and decided irrevocably.

It was raised anew in practice after October in many countries and in all possible forms and combinations, and everywhere it was settled the same way. A fundamental experience, following that of Kerenskyism, has been, as already mentioned, the Kuomintang experience. But no less importance is to be attached to the experience of fascism in Italy, where the petty-bourgeoisie, arms in hand, snatched the power from the old bourgeois parties in order to surrender it immediately, through its leaders, to the financial oligarchy. The same question arose in Poland, where the Pilsudski movement was aimed directly against the reactionary bourgeois-landlord government and mirrored the hopes of the petty-bourgeois masses and even of wide circles of the proletariat. It was no accident that the old Polish Social Democrat, Warski, out of fear of 'underestimating the peasantry', identified the **Pilsudski** revolution with the 'democratic dictatorship of the workers and peasants'. It would lead us too far a field, if I were to analyze here the Bulgarian experience, that is, the disgracefully confused policy of the Kolarovs and Kabakchievs towards tile party of Stambulisky, or the shameful experiment with the Farmer-Labour Party in the United States, or Zinoviev's romance with Radic, or the experience of the Communist Party of Rumania, and so on and so forth without end. Some of these facts are analyzed, in their essentials, in my *Criticism of the Draft Programme of the Communist International.* The fundamental conclusion of all these experiences fully confirms and strengthens the lessons of October-namely, that the petty-bourgeoisie, including the peasantry, is incapable of playing the role of leader in modern, even if backward, bourgeois society, in revolutionary no less than in reactionary epochs. The peasantry can either support the dictatorship of the bourgeoisie, or serve as prop to the dictatorship of the proletariat. Intermediate forms are only disguises for a dictatorship of the bourgeoisie, which has begun to totter or which has not yet recovered its feet after disturbances (Kerenskyism, Fascism, Pilsudski's regime).

The peasantry can follow either the bourgeoisie or the proletariat: But when the proletariat attempts to march at all costs with a peasantry which is not following it, the proletariat proves in fact to be tailing after finance capital: the workers as defenders of the fatherland in Russia in 1917; the workers—including the Communists as well—in the Kuomintang in China; the workers in the Polish Socialist Party, and also the Communists to some extent, in Poland in 1926, etc.

Whoever has not thought this out to the end, and who has not understood the events from the fresh trail they have left behind, had better not get involved in revolutionary politics.

The fundamental conclusion which Lenin drew from the lessons of the February and the October Revolutions, and drew exhaustively and comprehensively, thoroughly rejects the idea of the 'democratic dictatorship'. The following was repeated by Lenin more than once after 1918:

'The whole of political economy, if anybody has learned anything from it, the whole history of revolution, the whole history of political development throughout the nineteenth century, teaches us that the peasant follows the worker or the bourgeois .... If you do not know why, I would say to such citizens ....consider the development of any of the great revolutions of the eighteenth and nineteenth centuries, the political history of any country in the nineteenth century. It will tell you why. The economic structure of capitalist society is such that the ruling forces in it can only be capital or the proletariat which overthrows it. There are no other forces in the economic structure of that society.'

It is not a matter here of modern England or Germany. On the basis of the lessons of any one of the great revolutions of the eighteenth or the nineteenth centuries, that is, of the *bourgeois* revolutions in the *backward* countries, Lenin comes to the conclusion that only the dictatorship of the bourgeoisie or the dictatorship of the proletariat is possible. There cannot be a 'democratic', that is, an intermediate dictatorship.

His theoretical and historical excursion is summed up by Radek, as we see, in the rather thin aphorism that the bourgeois revolution must be distinguished from the socialist. Having descended to this 'step', Radek straightway stretches out a finger to Kuusinen who, proceeding from his one lone resource, that is, 'common sense', considers it improbable that the slogan of the proletarian dictatorship can be raised in both the advanced and the backward countries. With the sincerity of a man who understands nothing, Kuusinen convicts Trotsky of having 'learned nothing' since 1905. Following Kuusinen, Radek also becomes ironical: for Trotsky, 'the peculiarity of the Chinese and Indian revolutions consists precisely of the fact that they are in no way distinguished from the western European revolutions and must, therefore, in their first steps [?!] lead to the dictatorship of the proletariat.'

Radek forgets one trifle in this connection: The dictatorship of the proletariat was not realized in a Western European country, but precisely in a backward Eastern European country. Is it Trotsky's fault that the historical process overlooked the 'peculiarity' of Russia? Radek forgets further that the bourgeoisie—more accurately, finance capital—rules in all the capitalist countries, with all their diversity in level of development, social structure, traditions, etc., that is, all their 'peculiarities'. Here again, the lack of respect for this peculiarity proceeds from historical development and not at all from Trotsky.

Then wherein lies the distinction between the advanced and the backward countries? The distinction is great, but it still remains within the limits of the domination of capitalist relationships. The forms and methods of the rule of the bourgeoisie differ greatly in different countries. At one pole, the domination bears a stark and absolute character: *The United States*. At the other pole finance capital adapts itself to the outlived institutions of Asiatic medievalism by subjecting them to itself and imposing its own methods upon them: *India*. But the bourgeoisie rules in both places. From this it follows that the dictatorship of the proletariat also will have a highly varied character in terms of the social basis, the political forms, the immediate tasks and the tempo of work in the various capitalist countries. But to lead the masses of the people to victory over the bloc of the imperialists, the feudalists and the national bourgeoisie—this can be done only under the revolutionary hegemony of the proletariat, which transforms itself after the seizure of power into the dictatorship of the proletariat.

Radek fancies that when he has divided humanity into two groups—one which has 'matured' for the socialist dictatorship, and another which has 'matured' only for the democratic dictatorship—he has by this alone, in contrast to me, taken into consideration the alleged 'peculiarity' of the individual countries. In reality he has turned out a lifeless stereotype which can only divert the Communists from a genuine study of the peculiarity of a given country, i.e., the living interpenetration of the various steps and stages of historical development in that country.

The peculiarities of a country which has not accomplished or completed its democratic revolution are of such great significance that they must be taken as the basis for the program of the proletarian vanguard. Only upon the basis of such a national program can a Communist party develop its real and successful struggle for the majority of the working class and the toilers in general against the bourgeoisie and its democratic agents.

The possibility of success in this struggle is of course determined to a large extent by the role of the proletariat in the economy of the country, and consequently by the level of its capitalist development. This, however, is by no means the only criterion. No less important is the question whether a far-reaching and burning problem 'for the people' exists in the country, in the solution of which the majority of the nation is interested, and which demands for its solution the boldest revolutionary measures. Among problems of this kind are the agrarian question and the national question, in their varied combinations. With the acute agrarian problem and the intolerable national oppression in the colonial countries, the young and relatively small proletariat can come to power on the basis of a *national democratic* revolution sooner than the proletariat of an advanced country on a purely *socialist* basis. It might have seemed that since October there should be no necessity to prove this any more. But through the years of ideological reaction and through the theoretical depravity of the epigones, the elementary conceptions of the revolution have become so rank, so putrid and so.... Kuusinified, that one is compelled each time to begin all over again.

Does it follow from what has been said that all the countries of the world, in one way or another, are already today ripe for the socialist revolution? No, this is a false, dead, scholastic, Stalinist-Bukharinist way of putting the question. World economy in its entirety is indubitably ripe for socialism. But this does not mean that every country taken separately is ripe. Then what is to happen with the dictatorship of the proletariat in the various backward countries, in China, India, etc.? To this we answer: History is not made to order. A country can become 'ripe' for the dictatorship of the proletariat not only before it is ripe for the independent construction of socialism, but even before it is ripe for far-reaching socialization measures. One must not proceed from a preconceived harmony of social development. The law of uneven development still lives, despite the tender theoretical embraces of Stalin. The force of this law operates not only in the relations of countries to each other, but also in the mutual relationships of the various processes within one and the same country. A reconciliation of the uneven processes of economics and politics can be attained only on a world scale. In particular this means that the question of the dictatorship of the proletariat in China cannot be considered exclusively within the limits of Chinese economics and Chinese politics.

It is precisely here that we come up against the two mutually exclusive standpoints: the international revolutionary theory of the permanent revolution and the national-reformist theory of socialism in one country. Not only backward China, but in general no country in the world can build socialism within its own national limits: the 'highly-developed productive forces which have grown beyond national boundaries resist this, just as do those forces which are insufficiently developed for nationalization. The dictatorship of the proletariat in Britain, for example, will encounter difficulties and contradictions, different in character; it is true, but perhaps not slighter than those that will confront the dictatorship of the proletariat in China. Surmounting these contradictions is possible in both cases only by way of the international revolution. This standpoint leaves no room for the question of the 'maturity' or 'immaturity' of China for the socialist transformation. What remains indisputable here is that the backwardness of China makes the tasks of the proletarian dictatorship extremely difficult. But we repeat: History is not made to order, and the Chinese proletariat has no choice.

Does this at least mean that every country, including the most backward colonial country, is ripe, if not for socialism, then for the dictatorship of the proletariat? No, this is not what it means. Then what is to happen with the democratic revolution in general—and in the colonies in particular? Where is it written—I answer the question with another question—that every colonial country is ripe for the immediate and thoroughgoing solution of its national democratic tasks? The question must be approached from the other end. Under the conditions of the imperialist epoch the national democratic revolution can be carried through to a victorious end only when the social and political relationships of the country are mature for putting the proletariat in power as the leader of the masses of the people. And if this is not yet the case? Then the struggle for national liberation will produce only very partial results, results directed entirely against the working masses. In 1905, the proletariat of Russia did not prove strong enough to unite the peasant masses around it and to conquer power. For this very reason, the revolution halted midway, and then sank lower and lower. In China, where, in spite of the exceptionally favorable situation, the leadership of the Communist International prevented the Chinese proletariat from fighting for power, the national tasks found a wretched, unstable and niggardly solution in the regime of the Kuomintang.

When and under what conditions a colonial country will become ripe for the real revolutionary solution of its agrarian and national problems cannot be foretold. But in any case we can assert today with full certainty that not only China but also India will attain genuine people's democracy, that is, workers' and peasants' democracy, only through the dictatorship of the proletariat. On that road there may still be many stages, steps and phases. Under the pressure of the masses of the people the bourgeoisie will still take steps to the left, in order then to fall all the more mercilessly upon the people. Periods of dual power are possible and probable. But what there will not be, what there cannot be, is a genuine democratic dictatorship that is not the dictatorship of the proletariat. An 'independent' democratic dictatorship can only be of the type of the Kuomintang, that is, directed entirely against the workers and the peasants. We must understand this at the outset and teach it to the masses, without hiding the class realities behind abstract formulas.

Stalin and Bukharin preached that thanks to the yoke of imperialism the bourgeoisie could carry out the national revolution in China. The attempt was made. With what results? The proletariat was brought under the headman's axe. Then it was said: The democratic dictatorship will come next. The petty-bourgeois dictatorship proved to be only a masked dictatorship of capital. By accident? No. 'The peasant follows either the worker or the bourgeois.' In the first case, the dictatorship of the proletariat arises; in the other the dictatorship of the bourgeoisie. It would seem that the lesson of China is clear enough, even if studied from afar. 'No,' we are answered, 'that was merely an unsuccessful experiment. We will begin everything all over again and this time set up the " genuine " democratic dictatorship.' 'By what means?' 'On the social basis of the collaboration of the proletariat and the peasantry.' It is Radek who presents us with this latest discovery. But, if you will permit, the Kuomintang arose on that very same basis: workers and peasants 'collaborated'—to pull the chestnuts out of the fire for the bourgeoisie. Tell us what the political mechanics of this collaboration will look like. With what will you replace the Kuomintang? What parties will be in power? Indicate them at least approximately, at least describe them! To this Radek answers (in 1928!) that only people who are completely done for, who are incapable of understanding the complexity of Marxism, can be interested in such a secondary technical question as which class will be the horse and which the rider; whereas a Bolshevik must 'abstract' himself from the political superstructure, focusing his attention on the class foundation. No, permit me, you have already had your joke. You have already 'abstracted' enough. More than enough! In China, you 'abstracted' yourself from the question of how class collaboration expressed itself in party matters, you dragged the proletariat into the Kuomintang, you became infatuated with the Kuomintang to the point of losing your senses, you furiously resisted withdrawal from the Kuomintang; you shrank from political questions of struggle by repeating abstract formulas. And after the bourgeoisie has very concretely broken the skull of the proletariat, you propose to us: Let us try all over again; and as a beginning let us once more 'abstract' ourselves from the question of the parties and the revolutionary power. No! These are very poor jokes. We will not allow ourselves to be dragged back!

All these acrobatics, as we have perceived, are presented in the interest of an alliance of the workers and peasants. Radek warns the Opposition against an underestimation of the peasantry and cites the struggle of Lenin against the Mensheviks. Sometimes, when one observes what is being done with quotations from Lenin, one resents bitterly such offences against the dignity of human thought. Yes, Lenin said more than once that denial of the revolutionary role of the peasantry was characteristic of the Mensheviks. And that was right. But in addition to these quotations, there also was the year 1917, in which the Mensheviks spent the eight months which separated the February from the October Revolution in an unbroken bloc with the Socialist Revolutionaries. In that period the Socialist Revolutionaries represented the overwhelming majority of the peasantry awakened by the revolution. Together with the Socialist Revolutionaries, the Mensheviks called themselves the revolutionary democracy and remonstrated with us that they were the very ones who based themselves upon the alliance of the workers with the peasants (soldiers). Thus, after the February

Revolution the Mensheviks expropriated, so to speak, the Bolshevik formula of the alliance of the workers and peasants. The Bolsheviks were accused by them of wanting to split the proletarian vanguard from the peasantry and thereby to ruin the revolution. In other words, the **Mensheviks** accused Lenin of ignoring, or at least of underestimating the peasantry.

The criticism of Kamenev, Zinoviev and others directed against Lenin was only an echo of the criticism of the Mensheviks. The present criticism of Radek in turn is only a belated echo of the criticism of Kamenev.

The policy of the epigones in China, including Radek's policy, is the continuation and the further development of the Menshevik masquerade of 1917. The fact that the Communist party remained in the Kuomintang was defended not only by Stalin, but also by Radek, with the same reference to the necessity of the alliance of the workers and peasants. But when it was 'accidentally' revealed that the Kuomintang was a bourgeois party, the attempt was repeated with the 'Left' Kuomintang. The results were the same. Thereupon, the abstraction of the democratic dictatorship, in distinction from the dictatorship of the proletariat, was elevated above this sorry reality which had not fulfilled the high hopes—a fresh repetition of what we had already had. In 1917, we heard a hundred times from Tsereteli, Dan and the others: 'We already have the dictatorship of the revolutionary democracy, but you are driving toward the dictatorship of the proletariat, that is, toward ruin.' Truly, people have short memories. The 'revolutionary democratic dictatorship' of Stalin and Radek is in no way distinguished from the 'dictatorship of the revolutionary democracy' of Tsereteli and Dan. And in spite of that, this formula not only runs through all the resolutions of the Comintern, but it has also penetrated into its program. It is hard to conceive a more cunning masquerade and at the same time a more bitter revenge by Menshevism for the affronts which Bolshevism heaped upon it in 1917.

The revolutionists of the East, however, still have the right to demand a definite answer to the question of the character of the 'democratic dictatorship', based not upon old, *a priori* quotations, but upon facts and upon political experience. To the question: What is a 'democratic dictatorship'?—Stalin has repeatedly given the truly classical reply : For the East, it is approximately the same as 'Lenin conceived it with regard to the 1905 Revolution'. This has become the official formula to a certain extent. It can be found in the books and resolutions devoted to China, India or Polynesia. Revolutionists are referred to Lenin's 'conceptions' concerning *future* events, which in the meantime have long ago become *past* events, and in addition, the hypothetical 'conceptions' of Lenin are interpreted this way and that, but never in the way that Lenin himself interpreted them *after* the events.

'All right,' says the Communist of the East, hanging his head, 'we will try to conceive of it exactly as Lenin, according to your words, conceived of it before the revolution. But won't you please tell us what this slogan looks like in actuality? How was it realized in your country?'

'In our country it was realized in the shape of Kerenskyism in the epoch of dual power.'

'Can we tell our workers that the slogan of the democratic dictatorship will be realized in our country in the shape of in our own national Kerenskyism?'

'Come, come! Not at all! No worker will adopt such a slogan; Kerenskyism is servility to the bourgeoisie and betrayal of the working people.'

'But what, then, must we tell our workers?' the Communist of the East asks despondently.

'You must tell them,' impatiently answers Kuusinen, the man on duty, 'that the democratic dictatorship is the one that Lenin conceived of with regard to the future democratic revolution.'

If the Communist of the East is not lacking in sense, he will seek to rejoin:

'But didn't Lenin explain in 1918 that the democratic dictatorship found its genuine and true realization only in the October Revolution which established the dictatorship of the proletariat? Would it not be better to orient the party and the working class precisely toward this prospect?'

'Under no circumstances. Do not even dare to think about it. Why, that is the per-r-r-manent r-r-r-evolution! That's Tr-r-rotskyism!'

After this harsh reprimand the Communist of the East turns paler than the snow on the highest peaks of the Himalayas and abandons any further craving for knowledge. Let whatever will happen, happen!

And the consequences? We know them well: either contemptible grovelling before Chiang Kai-shek, or heroic adventures.

Notes

1. Chiang Kai-shek is the leader of the Right Wing, and Wang Ching-wei of the Left Wing of the Kuomintang. Tang Ping-shan served as a Cornmunist Minister, carrying out the line of Stalin and Bukharin in China.-- L.T.

CHAPTER EIGHT

FROM MARXISM TO PACIFISM

What is most alarming, as a symptom, is a passage in Radek's article which, to be sure, seems to stand apart from the central theme that interests us, but which is intimately bound up with this theme by the uniformity of Radek's shift toward the present theoreticians of centrism. I refer to the somewhat disguised advances he makes toward the theory of socialism in one country. One must dwell on this, for this 'side-line' of Radek's errors can surpass all the other differences of opinion in its further development, revealing that their quantity has definitively turned into quality.

Discussing the dangers that threaten the revolution from without, Radek writes that Lenin ' .... was conscious of the fact that *with the level of economic development in Russia in 1905* this [the proletarian] dictatorship can maintain itself only if the Western European proletariat comes to its aid'. (My emphasis—L.T.).
One mistake after another; above all, a very crude violation of the historical perspective. In reality Lenin said, and that more than once, that the democratic dictatorship (and not at all the proletarian) in

Russia would be unable to maintain itself without the socialist revolution in Europe. This idea runs like a red thread through all the articles and speeches of Lenin in the days of the Stockholm party congress in 1906 (polemic against Plekhanov, questions of nationalization, etc.). In that period, Lenin did not even raise the question of a proletarian dictatorship in Russia before the socialist revolution in Western Europe. But it is not there that the most important thing lies for the moment. What is the meaning of 'with the level of economic development of Russia in 1905'? And how do matters stand with the level in 1917? It is on this difference in levels that the theory of socialism in one country is erected. The program of the Comintern has divided the whole globe into squares which are 'adequate' in level for the independent construction of socialism and others which are 'inadequate'; and has thus created for revolutionary strategy a series of hopeless blind alleys. Differences in economic levels can undoubtedly be of decisive significance for the political power of the working class. In 1905, we could not raise ourselves to the dictatorship of the proletariat, just as, for that matter, we were unable to rise to the democratic dictatorship. In 1917 we set up the dictatorship of the proletariat, which swallowed up the democratic dictatorship. But with the economic development of 1917 just as with the 1905 level the dictatorship can maintain itself and develop to socialism only if the Western European proletariat comes opportunely to its assistance Naturally, this 'opportune-ness' cannot be calculated *a priori* ; it is determined in the course of development and struggle. As against this *fundamental* question, determined by the *world* relationship of forces, which has the last and decisive word, the difference between levels of development of Russia in 1905 and in 1917, however important it is in itself, is a factor of the secondary order.

But Radek does not content himself with the ambiguous reference to this difference of levels. After referring to the fact that Lenin saw the connection between the internal problems of the revolution and its world problems (well, now!) Radek adds:

'But Lenin did not *sharpen* only the concept of this connection between the maintenance of the socialist dictatorship in Russia and aid from the Western European proletariat, as it was *excessively sharpened by Trotsky's formulation*, namely, that it must be *state* aid, that is, the aid of the already victorious Western European proletariat.' (My emphasis—L.T.).

Frankly, I did not trust my eyes when I read these lines. To what end did Radek require this worthless weapon from the arsenal of the epigones? This is simply a shamefaced rehash of the Stalinist banalities which we always used to make such thorough game of. Apart from everything else, the quotation shows that Radek has a very poor notion of the fundamental landmarks of Lenin's path. Lenin, unlike Stalin, not only never contrasted the pressure of the European proletariat upon the bourgeois power to the capture of power by the proletariat; on the contrary, he formulated the question of revolutionary aid from without much more sharply than I. In the epoch of the first revolution, he repeated tirelessly that we should not retain democracy (not even democracy!) without the socialist revolution in Europe. Generally speaking, in 1917-18 and the years that followed, Lenin did not consider and estimate the fate of our revolution in any way other than in connection with the socialist revolution that had begun in Europe. He asserted openly, for example: 'Without the victory of the revolution in Germany, we are doomed.' He said this in 1918, that is, *not* with the 'economic level' of 1905 ; and he had in mind not future decades, but the period immediately ahead, which was a matter of a few years, if not months.

Lenin dozens of times: If we have held out 'the reason .... was that a fortunate combination of circumstances protected us for a short time from international imperialism' (for a short time!—L.T.). And further: 'International imperialism could not under any circumstances, on any condition, live side by side with the Soviet Republic..... In this sphere conflict is inevitable.' And the conclusion? Isn't it the pacifist hope in the 'pressure' of the proletariat or in the 'neutralization' of the bourgeoisie? No, the conclusion reads: 'Here lies the greatest difficulty of the Russian Revolution .... the necessity of calling forth an international revolution.' When was this said and written? Not in 1905, when Nicholas II negotiated with Wilhelm II on the suppression of the revolution and when I advanced my 'sharpened' formula, but in 1918, 1919 and the following years.

Here is what Lenin said, looking back, at the Third Congress of the Comintern:

'It was clear to us that without the support of the international world revolution the victory of the proletarian revolution [in Russia—L.T.]

was impossible. Before the revolution and even after it, we thought: Either revolution breaks out in the other countries, in the capitalistically more developed countries, immediately, or at least very quickly, or we must perish. Notwithstanding this conviction, we did all we possibly could to preserve the Soviet system under all circumstances, come what may, because we knew that we were working not only for ourselves but also for the international revolution. We knew this, we repeatedly expressed this conviction before the October Revolution, immediately afterward, and at the time we signed the Brest-Litovsk Treaty. *And, speaking generally, this was correct.* In actual fact, however, events did not proceed along as straight a line as we expected.' (*Minutes of the Third Congress of the Comintern*, Russian edition).

From 1921 onward, the movement began to proceed along a line that was not so straight as I, together with Lenin, had expected in 1917-19 (and not only in 1905). But it nevertheless did develop along the line of the irreconcilable contradictions between the workers' state and the bourgeois world. One of the two must perish! The workers' state can be preserved from mortal dangers, not only military but also economic, only by the victorious development of the proletarian revolution in the West. The attempt to discover two positions, Lenin's and mine, on this question, is the height of theoretical slovenliness. At least re-read Lenin, do not slander him, do not feed us with stale Stalinist mush!

But the plunge downward does not stop even here. After Radek inventing the story that Lenin considered adequate the 'simple' (in essence, reformist, Purcellian) aid of the world proletariat, while Trotsky 'exaggeratedly demanded' only state aid, that is, revolutionary aid, Radek continues :

'Experience showed that *on this point, too,* Lenin was right, The European proletariat was not yet able to capture power, but it was strong enough, during the intervention, to prevent the world bourgeoisie from throwing substantial forces against us. Thereby it helped us maintain the Soviet power. Fear of the labor movement, along with the antagonisms in the capitalist world itself, was the main force that has guaranteed the maintenance of peace during the eight years, since the end of the intervention.'

This passage, while it does not sparkle with originality against the background of the exercises written by the literary functionaries of our time, is nevertheless noteworthy for its combination of historical anachronisms, political confusion and the grossest errors of principle.

From Radek's words it would follow that Lenin in 1905 foretold in his pamphlet *Two Tactics* (this is the only work to which Radek refers) that the relationship of forces between states and classes after 1917 would be such as to exclude for a long time the possibility of a large-scale military intervention against us. In contrast to this, Trotsky in 1905 did not foresee the situation that would necessarily arise after the imperialist war, but only reckoned with the realities of that time, such as the mighty Hohenzollern army, the very strong Hapsburg army, the mighty French Bourse, etc. This is truly a monstrous anachronism, which becomes even more complicated by its ridiculous inner contradictions. For, according to Radek, my principal mistake consisted precisely of the fact that I did put forward the prospect of the dictatorship of the proletariat 'with the level of development of 1905'. Now the second mistake becomes plain: I did not consider the prospect of the dictatorship of the proletariat put forward by me on the eve of the 1905 Revolution in the light of the international situation which arose only after 1917. When Stalin's usual arguments look like this, we don't wonder about it, for we know well enough his 'level of development', in 1917 as well as in 1928. But how did Radek fall into such company?

Yet even this is not yet the worst. The worst lies in the fact that Radek has skipped over the boundary that separates Marxism from opportunism, the revolutionary from the pacifist position. It is a question of nothing less than the struggle against war, that is, of *how and with what methods war can be averted or stopped; by the pressure of the proletariat upon the bourgeoisie or by civil war to overthrow the bourgeoisie?* Radek has unwittingly introduced a fundamental question of proletarian policy into the controversy between us.

Does Radek want to say that I 'ignore' not only the peasantry but also the pressure of the proletariat upon the bourgeoisie, and have taken into consideration the proletarian revolution exclusively? It is hardly to be assumed that he will defend such an absurdity, worthy of a Thaelmann, a Semard or a Monnosseau. At the Third Congress of the

Comintern, the ultra-lefts of that time (Zinoviev, Thalheimer, Thaelmann, Bela Kun, etc.) advocated tactics of putschism in the West in order to save the USSR. Together with Lenin, I explained to them as popularly as possible that the best possible assistance they could render us would be systematically and in a planned way to consolidate their positions and prepare themselves for the capture of power, instead of improvising revolutionary adventures for our sakes. At that time, regrettably enough, Radek was not on the side of Lenin and Trotsky, but on the side of Zinoviev and Bukharin. But Radek surely recollects—at any rate, the minutes of the Third Congress recollect it—that the essence of the argument of Lenin and myself consisted precisely of assailing the irrationally 'sharpened formulation' of the ultra-lefts. After we had explained to them that the strengthening of the party and the pressure of the proletariat are very serious factors in internal and international relations, we Marxists added that 'pressure' is only a function of the revolutionary struggle for power and depends entirely upon the development of this struggle. For this reason, Lenin delivered a speech at the end of the Third Congress, at a big private session of the delegates, which was directed against tendencies to passivity and waiting upon events, and closed with approximately the following moral: Engage in no adventures, but, dear friends, please do not tarry, for with 'pressure' alone we cannot last long.

Radek refers to the fact that the European proletariat was not able to take power after the war, but that it prevented the bourgeoisie from crushing us. I also had more than one occasion to speak of this. Nevertheless, the European proletariat succeeded in preventing our destruction only because the pressure of the proletariat coincided with the very grave objective consequences of the imperialist war and the world antagonisms aggravated by it. It is impossible to say which of these elements was of more decisive significance: the struggle within the imperialist camp, the economic collapse, or the pressure of the proletariat; but the question cannot be put in that way. That peaceful pressure alone is inadequate was demonstrated too clearly by the imperialist war, which came in spite of all 'pressure'. And finally, and this is most important, if the pressure of the proletariat in the first, most critical years of the Soviet Republic proved to be effective enough, then it was only because at that time for the workers of

Europe it was not a question of exerting pressure, but of struggling for power—and this struggle repeatedly assumed the form of civil war.

In 1905, there was neither a war nor an economic collapse in Europe, and capitalism and militarism were in full-blooded frenzy. The 'pressure' of the Social Democrats of that time was absolutely incapable of preventing Wilhelm II or Franz Josef from marching into the Kingdom of Poland with their troops, or, in general, from coming to the aid of the Tsar. And even in 1918, the pressure of the German proletariat did not prevent Hohenzollern from occupying the Baltic provinces and the Ukraine, and if he did not get as far as Moscow then it was only because his military forces were not adequate. Otherwise, how and why did we conclude the Brest peace? How easily yesterday is forgotten! Lenin did not confine himself to hope for 'pressure' by the proletariat, but repeatedly asserted that without revolution in Germany we should certainly perish. This was correct in essence, although a greater period of time has intervened. Let there be no illusions; we have received an undated moratorium. We live, as before, under the conditions of a 'breathing-space'.

A condition in which the proletariat is as yet unable to seize power, but can prevent the bourgeoisie from utilizing its power for a war, is a condition of unstable class equilibrium in its highest expression. An equilibrium is called unstable precisely when it cannot last long. It must tip toward one side or the other. Either the proletariat comes to power or else the bourgeoisie, by a series of crushing blows, weakens the revolutionary pressure sufficiently to regain freedom of action, above all in the question of war and peace.

Only a reformist can picture the pressure of the proletariat upon the bourgeois state as a permanently increasing factor and as a guarantee against intervention. It is precisely out of this conception that arose the theory of the construction of socialism in one country, given the *neutralization* of the world bourgeoisie (Stalin). Just as the owl takes flight at twilight, so also did the Stalinist theory of the neutralization of the bourgeoisie by the pressure of the proletariat arise only when the conditions which engendered this theory had begun to disappear.

The world situation underwent abrupt changes in the period when the falsely interpreted postwar experience led to the deceptive hope that we could get along without the revolution of the European proletariat by substituting for it 'support' in general. The defeats of the proletariat have paved the way for capitalist stabilization. The collapse of capitalism after the war has been overcome. New generations have grown up that have not tasted the horrors of the imperialist slaughter. The result is that the bourgeoisie is now freer to dispose of its war machine than it was five or eight years ago.

As the working masses move to the Left, this process will undoubtedly, as it develops further, once more increase their pressure upon the bourgeois state. But this is a two-edged factor. It is precisely the growing danger from the side of the working class that can, at a later stage, drive the bourgeoisie to decisive steps in order 90 shows that it is master in its own house, and to attempt to destroy the main centre of contagion, the Soviet Republic. *The struggle against war is decided not by pressure upon the government but only by the revolutionary struggle for power.* The 'pacifist' effects of the proletarian class struggle, like its reformist effects, are only by-products of the revolutionary struggle for power; they have only a relative strength and can easily turn into their opposite, that is, they can drive the bourgeoisie to take the road to war. The bourgeoisie's fear of the labor movement, to which Radek refers so one-sidedly, is the most substantial hope of all social-pacifists. But 'fear' of the revolution alone decides nothing. The revolution decides. For this reason, Lenin said in 1905 that the only guarantee against the monarchist restoration, and, in 1918, against the restoration of capitalism, is not the pressure of the proletariat but its revolutionary victory in Europe. This is the only correct way of putting the question. In spite of the lengthy character of the 'breathing-space', Lenin's formulation retains its full force even today. I, too, formulated the question in the very same way. I wrote in *Results and Prospects* in 1906:

'It is precisely the fear of the revolt of the proletariat that compels the bourgeois parties, even while voting monstrous sums for military expenditure, to make solemn declarations in favor of peace, to dream of International Arbitration Courts and even of the organization of a United States of Europe. These pitiful declamations can, of course, abolish neither the antagonism between states nor armed conflicts.' (*Our Revolution*, 'Results and Prospects'.)

The basic mistake of the Sixth Congress lies in this, that in order to save the pacifist and national-reformist perspectives of Stalin-Bukharin, it ran after revolutionary-technical recipes against the war danger, separating the struggle against war from the struggle for power.

The inspirers of the Sixth Congress, these alarmed builders of socialism in one country—in essence, frightened pacifists—made the attempt to perpetuate the 'neutralization' of the bourgeoisie through intensified 'pressure' methods. But since they couldn't help knowing that their leadership up to now in a series of countries had led to the defeat of the revolution and had thrown the international vanguard of the proletariat far back, they endeavored first of all to jettison the 'sharpened formulation' of Marxism, which indissolubly ties up the problem of war with the problem of the revolution. They have converted the struggle against war into a self-sufficient task. Lest the national parties oversleep the decisive hour, they have proclaimed the war danger to be permanent, unpostponable and immediate. Everything that happens in the world happens for the purpose of war. War is now no longer an instrument of the bourgeois regime; the bourgeois regime is an instrument of war. As a consequence, the struggle of the Communist International against war is converted into a system of ritualistic formulas, which are repeated automatically on every occasion and, losing their effectiveness, evaporate. Stalinist national socialism tends to convert the Communist International into an auxiliary means of 'pressure' upon the bourgeoisie. It is just this tendency, and not Marxism, that Radek helps with his hasty, slovenly, superficial criticism. He has lost the compass and has got into a strange current that may carry him to far different shores.

Alma-Ata, October 1928

EPILOGUE

The prediction, or apprehension which I expressed in the concluding lines of the previous chapter was, as the reader knows, confirmed a few months later. The criticism of the permanent revolution only served Radek as a lever to push himself away from the Opposition. Our whole book proves, we hope, that Radek's passage into the camp of Stalin did not come to us unexpectedly. But even apostasy has its gradations, its levels of debasement. In his declaration of repentance, Radek completely rehabilitates Stalin's policy in China. This means plumbing the lowest depths of betrayal. It only remains for me to quote an extract from my reply to the declaration of penitence by Radek, Preobrazhensky and Smilga, which puts them on the black list of political cynics:

'As befits all self-respecting bankrupts, the trio has not of course failed to take cover behind the permanent revolution. The most tragic experience of the whole recent history of the defeats of opportunism— the Chinese Revolution—this trio of capitulators seeks to dismiss with a cheap oath guaranteeing that it has nothing in common with the theory of the permanent revolution.

'Radek and Smilga obstinately defended the subordination of the Chinese Communist Party to the bourgeois Kuomintang, not only up to Chiang Kai-shek's coup d'etat but also afterwards. Preobrazhensky mumbled something inarticulate, as he always does when political questions are involved. A remarkable fact: all those in the ranks of the Opposition who defended the subordination of the Communist Party to the Kuomintang turned out to be capitulators. Not a single Oppositionist who remained true to his banner bears this mark, which is a mark of notorious shame. Three-quarters of a century after the appearance of the Communist Manifesto, a quarter of a century after the founding of the party of the Bolsheviks, these ill-starred "Marxists" considered it possible to defend the keeping of the Communists in the cage of the Kuomintang! In his answer to my charges, Radek already then, just as in his letter of repentence today, tried to frighten us with the "isolation " of the proletariat from the peasantry in the event of the Communist Party's withdrawing from the bourgeois Kuomintang. Shortly before that, Radek called the Canton government a peasants' and workers' government and thereby helped Stalin to disguise the subordination of the proletariat to the bourgeoisie. With what are these shameful deeds, the consequences of this blindness, this stupidity, this betrayal of Marxism, to be covered? With what, indeed! With an indictment of the permanent revolution!

'As far back as February 1928, Radek, who was already looking for pretexts for his capitulation, adhered promptly to the resolution on the Chinese question adopted by the February 1928 Plenum of the Executive Committee of the Comintern. This resolution brands the Trotskyites as liquidators because they called defeats and were not willing to consider the victorious Chinese counterrevolution as the highest stage of the Chinese Revolution. In this February resolution the course towards armed uprising and Soviets was proclaimed. For every person not entirely devoid of political sense and tempered by revolutionary experience, this resolution constituted an example of the most revolting and most irresponsible adventurism. Radek adhered to it. Preobrazhensky approached the matter no less ingeniously than Radek, only from the opposite end. The Chinese Revolution, he wrote, is already defeated, and defeated for a long time. A new revolution will not come soon. Is it worth while squabbling about China with the centrists? On this theme, Preobrazhensky sent out lengthy ep•istles. When I read them in Alma-Ata, I experienced a feeling of shame. What did these people learn in the school of Lenin? I asked myself over and over again. Preobrazhensky's premises were diametrically opposed to Radek's premises, yet the conclusions were the same: both of them were inspired by the great desire for Yaroslavsky to embrace them fraternally through the good offices of Menzhinsky. Oh, of course, they did it for the good of the revolution. These are not careerists. Not at all. They are simply helpless, ideologically bankrupt individuals.

'To the adventurist resolution of the February Plenum of the ECCI (1928) I already then counter-posed a course towards the mobilization of the Chinese workers under democratic slogans, including the slogan of a Constituent Assembly for China. But here the ill-starred trio fell into ultra-leftism; that was cheap and committed them to nothing. Democratic slogans? Never. "This is a gross mistake on Trotsky's part". Only soviets for China -- not a farthing less! It is hard to conceive of anything more senseless than this—by your leave—position. The slogan of soviets for an epoch of bourgeois reaction is a baby's rattle, i.e., a mockery of soviets. But even in the epoch of revolution, that is, in the epoch of the direct building of soviets, we did not withdraw the democratic slogans. We did not withdraw them until the real soviets, which had already conquered power, clashed before the eyes of the masses with the real institutions of democracy. This signifies in the language of Lenin (and not of the philistine Stalin and his parrots): not skipping over the democratic stage in the development of the country.

'Without the democratic program—constituent assembly, eight-hour day, confiscation of the land, national independence of China, right of self-determination for the peoples living within it—without this democratic program, the Communist Party of China is bound hand and foot and is compelled to surrender the field passively to the Chinese

Social-Democrats who may, with the aid of Stalin, Radek and company, assume the place of the Communist Party.

'Thus: although following in the wake of the Opposition, Radek nevertheless missed what was most important in the Chinese Revolution, for he defended the subordination of the Communist Party to the bourgeois Kuomintang. Radek missed the Chinese counter-revolution, supporting the course toward armed uprising after the Canton adventure. Radek today skips over the period of the counter-revolution and the struggle for democracy by waving aside the tasks of the transition period in favor of the most abstract idea of soviets outside of time and space. But in return Radek swears that he has nothing in common with the permanent revolution. That is gratifying. That is consoling.....

'The anti-Marxist theory of Stalin and Radek means for China, India and all the countries of the East, an altered but not improved repetition of the Kuomintang experiment.

'On the basis of all the experience of the Russian and Chinese Revolution, on the basis of the teachings of Marx and Lenin, tested in the light of these revolutions, the Opposition affirms:

'That the new Chinese revolution can overthrow the existing regime and transfer the power to the masses of the people only in the form of the dictatorship of the proletariat :

'That the "democratic dictatorship of the proletariat and the peasantry", in contrast to the dictatorship of the proletariat which leads the peasantry and realizes the program of democracy, is a fiction, a self-deception, or what is worse still—Kerenskyism or Kuomintangism.

'Between the regime of Kerensky and Chiang Kai-shek, on the one hand, and the dictatorship of the proletariat on the other, there is no half-way, intermediate revolutionary regime and there can be none. Whoever puts forward the bare formula of such a regime is shamefully deceiving the workers of the East and is preparing new catastrophes.

'The Opposition says to the workers of the East: Bankrupted by the inner-party machinations, the capitulators are helping Stalin to sow the seeds of centrism, to throw sand in your eyes, to stop up your ears, to befuddle your heads. On the one hand, you are rendered helpless in the face of stark bourgeois dictatorship by being forbidden to engage in a struggle for democracy. On the other hand, there is unrolled before you a panorama of some sort of saving, non-proletarian dictatorship, which facilitates a fresh reincarnation of the Kuomintang in the future, that is, further defeats for the workers' and peasants' revolution.

'Such preachers are betrayers. Learn to distrust them, workers of the East; learn to despise them, learn to drive them out of your ranks! ....

WHAT IS THE PERMANENT REVOLUTION?

Basic Postulates

I hope that the reader will not object if, to end this book, I attempt, without fear of repetition, to formulate succinctly my principal conclusions.

1. The theory of the permanent revolution now demands the greatest attention from every Marxist, for the course of the class and ideological struggle has fully and finally raised this question from the realm of reminiscences over old differences of opinion among Russian Marxists, and converted it into a question of the character, the inner connexions and methods of the international revolution in general.

2. With regard to countries with a belated bourgeois development, especially the colonial and semi-colonial countries, the theory of the permanent revolution signifies that the complete and genuine solution of their tasks of achieving *democracy and national emancipation* is conceivable only through the dictatorship of the proletariat as the leader of the subjugated nation, above all of its peasant masses.

3. Not only the agrarian, but also the national question assigns to the peasantry—the overwhelming majority of the population in backward countries—an exceptional place in the democratic revolution. Without an alliance of the proletariat with the peasantry the tasks of the democratic revolution cannot be solved, nor even seriously posed. But the alliance of these two classes can be realized in no other way than through an irreconcilable struggle against the influence of the national-liberal bourgeoisie.

4. No matter what the first episodic stages of the revolution may be in the individual countries, the realization of the revolutionary alliance between the proletariat and the peasantry is conceivable only under the political leadership of the proletariat vanguard, organized in the Communist Party. This in turn means that the victory of the democratic revolution is conceivable only through the dictatorship of the proletariat which bases itself upon the alliance with the peasantry and solves first of all the tasks of the democratic revolution.

5. Assessed historically, the old slogan of Bolshevism—'the democratic dictatorship of the proletariat and peasantry'—expressed precisely the above-characterized relationship of the proletariat, the peasantry and the liberal bourgeoisie. This has been confirmed by the experience of October. But Lenin's old formula did not settle in advance the problem of what the reciprocal relations would be between the proletariat and the peasantry within the revolutionary bloc. In other words, the formula deliberately retained a certain algebraic quality, which had to make way for more precise arithmetical quantities in the process of historical experience. However, the latter showed, and under circumstances that exclude any kind of misinterpretation, that no matter how great the revolutionary role of the peasantry may be, it nevertheless cannot be an independent role and even less a leading one. The peasant follows either the worker or the bourgeois. This means that the 'democratic dictatorship of the proletariat and peasantry' is only conceivable as a *dictatorship of the proletariat that leads the peasant masses behind it.*

6. A democratic dictatorship of the proletariat and peasantry, as a regime that is distinguished from the dictatorship of the proletariat by its class content, might be realized only in a case where an *independent* revolutionary party could be constituted, expressing the interests of the peasants and in general of petty bourgeois democracy— a party capable of conquering power with this or that degree of aid from the proletariat, and of determining its revolutionary program. As all modern history attests—especially the Russian experience of the last twenty-five years—an insurmountable obstacle on the road to the creation of a peasants' party is the petty-bourgeoisie's lack of economic and political independence and its deep internal differentiation. By reason of this the upper sections of the petty-bourgeoisie (of the peasantry) go along with the big bourgeoisie in all decisive cases, especially in war and in revolution; the lower sections go along with the proletariat; the intermediate section being thus compelled to choose between the two extreme poles. Between Kerenskyism and the Bolshevik power, between the Kuomintang and the dictatorship of the proletariat, there is not and cannot be any intermediate stage, that is, no democratic dictatorship of the workers and peasants.

7. The Comintern's endeavor to foist upon the Eastern countries the slogan of the democratic dictatorship of the proletariat and peasantry, finally and long ago exhausted by history, can have only a reactionary effect. Insofar as this slogan is counter-posed to the slogan of the dictatorship of the proletariat, it contributes politically to the dissolution of the proletariat in the petty-bourgeois masses and thus creates the most favorable conditions for the hegemony of the national bourgeoisie and consequently for the collapse of the democratic revolution. The introduction of the slogan into the program of the Comintern is a direct betrayal of Marxism and of the October tradition of Bolshevism.

8. The dictatorship of the proletariat which has risen to power as the leader of the democratic revolution is inevitably and, very quickly confronted with tasks, the fulfillment of which is bound up with deep inroads into the rights of bourgeois property. The democratic revolution grows over directly into the socialist revolution and thereby becomes a *permanent* revolution.

9. The conquest of power by the proletariat does not complete the revolution, but only opens it. Socialist construction is conceivable only on the foundation of the class struggle, on a national and international scale. This struggle, under the conditions of an overwhelming predominance of capitalist relationships on the world arena, must inevitably lead to explosions, that is, internally to civil wars and externally to revolutionary wars. Therein lies the permanent character of the socialist revolution as such, regardless of whether it is a backward country that is involved, which only yesterday accomplished its democratic revolution, or an old capitalist country which already has behind it a long epoch of democracy and parliamentarism.

10. The completion of the socialist revolution within national limits is unthinkable. One of the basic reasons for the crisis in bourgeois society is the fact that the productive forces created by it can no longer be reconciled with the framework of the national state. From this follows on the one hand, imperialist wars, on the other, the utopia of a bourgeois United States of Europe. The socialist revolution begins on the national arena, it unfolds on the international arena, and is completed on the world arena. Thus, the socialist revolution becomes a permanent revolution in a newer and broader sense of the word; it attains completion, only in the final victory of the new society on our entire planet.

11. The above-outlined sketch of the development of the world revolution eliminates the question of countries that are 'mature' or 'immature' for socialism in the spirit of that pedantic, lifeless classification given by the present program of the Comintern. Insofar as capitalism has created a world market, a world division of labor and world productive forces, it has also prepared world economy as a whole for socialist transformation.

Different countries will go through this process at different tempos. Backward countries may, under certain conditions, arrive at the dictatorship of the proletariat sooner than advanced countries, but they will come later than the latter to socialism.

A backward colonial or semi-colonial country, the proletariat of which is insufficiently prepared to unite the peasantry and take power, is thereby incapable of bringing the democratic revolution to its conclusion. Contrariwise, in a country where the proletariat has power in its hands as the result of the democratic revolution, the subsequent fate of the dictatorship and socialism depends in the last analysis not only and not so much upon the national productive forces as upon the development of the international socialist revolution.

12. The theory of socialism in one country, which rose on the yeast of the reaction against October, is the only theory that consistently and to the very end opposes the theory of the permanent revolution.

The attempt of the epigones, under the lash of our criticism, to confine the application of the theory of socialism in one country exclusively to Russia, because of its specific characteristics (its vastness and its natural resources), does not improve matters but only makes them worse. The break with the internationalist position always and invariably leads to national messianism, that is, to attributing special superiorities and qualities to one's own country, which allegedly permit it to play a role to which other countries cannot attain.

The world division of labor, the dependence of Soviet industry upon foreign technology, the dependence of the productive forces of the advanced countries of Europe upon Asiatic raw materials, etc., etc., make the construction of an independent socialist society in any single country in the world impossible.

13. The theory of Stalin and Bukharin, running counter to the entire experience of the Russian revolution, not only sets up the democratic revolution mechanically in contrast to the socialist revolution, but also makes a breach between the national revolution and the international revolution.

This theory imposes upon revolutions in backward countries the task of establishing an unrealizable regime of democratic dictatorship, which it counter-poses to the dictatorship of the proletariat. Thereby this theory introduces illusions and fictions into politics, paralyses the struggle for power of the proletariat in the East, and hampers the victory of the colonial revolution.

The very seizure of power by the proletariat signifies, from the standpoint of the epigones' theory, the completion of the revolution ('to the extent of nine-tenths', according to Stalin's formula) and the opening of the epoch of national reforms. The theory of the kulak growing into socialism and the theory of the 'neutralization' of the world bourgeoisie are consequently inseparable from the theory of socialism in one country. They stand or fall together.

By the theory of national socialism, the Communist International is down-graded to an auxiliary weapon useful only for the struggle against military intervention. The present policy of the Comintern, its regime and the selection of its leading personnel correspond entirely to the demotion of the Communist International to the role of an auxiliary unit which is not destined to solve independent tasks.

14. The program of the Comintern created by Bukharin is eclectic through and through. It makes the hopeless attempt to reconcile the theory of socialism in one country with Marxist internationalism, which is, however, inseparable from the permanent character of the world revolution. The struggle of the Communist Left Opposition for a correct policy and a healthy regime in the Communist International is inseparably bound up with the struggle for the Marxist program. The question of the program is in turn inseparable from the question of the two mutually exclusive theories: the theory of permanent revolution and the theory of socialism in one country. The problem of the permanent revolution has long ago outgrown the episodic differences of opinion between Lenin and Trotsky, which were completely exhausted by history. The struggle is between the basic ideas of Marx and Lenin on the one side and the eclecticism of the centrists on the other.

Made in the USA
Monee, IL
03 September 2022